Praise for
What Your Customer Wants and Can't Tell You

"You trust your gut, right? Well, so did many other business leaders, just before their gut reactions led them to make decisions that brought down great companies and high-flying careers. Melina Palmer's book, relying on the latest research in behavioral economics, shows you how to avoid the dangerous judgment errors called cognitive biases that brought down previously successful leaders. Palmer is an excellent science and business communicator and provides clear and business-relevant explanations of what you need to know to use behavioral economics insights to protect your company and career."

—Dr. Gleb Tsipursky, behavioral scientist, CEO of Disaster Avoidance Experts and bestselling author of *Never Go with Your Gut* and *The Blindspots Between Us*

"Melina is skilled in taking the theoretical concepts behind behavioral economics and making them easy to understand and apply. She is a thought leader in this space, experienced at working with marketing and non-marketing professionals in integrating these concepts into their corporate strategy and driving significant results. This book is a must have for anyone that is looking to grow their business through a deeper understanding of how people make decisions."

—Justin Martin, EVP/chief operating officer of Verity Credit Union

"With this book, Melina will challenge the way you think about your personal and business decisions and the real 'whys' driving your customers' choices. Don't 'overthink' this decision to dig in and learn."

—Will Leach, CEO of Mindstate Group
and author of *Marketing to Mindstates*

"*What Your Customer Wants and Can't Tell You: Unlocking Consumer Brains with the Science of Behavioral Economics* is a great guide to the customer's mind. Written for the savvy businessperson, the book delves into behavioral economics with an entry-level, yet accessible, approach that will not only enlighten, but also entertain."

—Nir Eyal, bestselling author of *Hooked* and *Indistractable*

"Melina Palmer has taken the insights she has gathered from years of producing her wonderful podcast, *The Brainy Business*, and packed them all into this fun, delightful book that will leave you with new, smart ideas to launch your business to the next level. Filled with actionable knowledge, *What Your Customer Wants and Can't Tell You: Unlocking Consumer Brains with the Science of Behavioral Economics* is a treasure trove of ways you can use psychological principles to amplify your marketing and sales efforts. From insights on pricing and priming, to messaging and nudges, to reciprocity and habits, this book provides you with hundreds of hints and tips that can be implemented immediately. This is a must-read for anyone who is interested in how to unlock the power of behavioral economics with their customers."

—Dr. Kurt Nelson, founder and chief behavioral scientist of The Lantern Group and cohost of the award-winning *Behavioral Grooves* podcast

"I really enjoyed reading *What Your Customer Wants and Can't Tell You*. Melina is a great storyteller and, being a twenty-four-year P&G Insights veteran, I can see how most (if not all) of these behavioral economics concepts have been applied to the different brands I've worked on. *What Your Customer Wants and Can't Tell You* pulls these concepts together beautifully by providing case studies and stories, making it far easier than any other resources I've seen to translate BE concepts into a world of business."

—Dr. D. Keith Ewart, VP Insights at CloudArmy

"Melina Palmer, a true expert in the field of behavioral economics, has developed a comprehensive and digestible must-read for everyone who works with brands—from CEO to marketing staff, product developer to solopreneur, and everyone in between. Anyone interested in leadership and running a successful, profitable business should get a copy of *What Your Customer Wants and Can't Tell You* and share it with their teams immediately."

—Cristina McLamb, founder and CEO of Niche Skincare

"*What Your Customer Wants and Can't Tell You* is a superb, easy-to-read exposé of how to apply key behavioral principles. Told in a very compelling way with an authentic style, it is a terrific guide for marketers and industry practitioners the world over. Anyone in business would benefit from the insights in this book."

—Nuala Walsh, founder of MINDEQUITY, vice-chair of UN Women UK, and cofounding member of the Global Association of Applied Behavioral Scientists

"Melina Palmer's book *What Your Customer Wants and Can't Tell You* is a wonderful guide full of behavioral economics principles and insights that can be applied in your everyday work, and an exceptional companion to Melina's podcast, *The Brainy Business*. A one-two punch that will be sure to 'nudge' you into the wonderful world of applied behavior science."

—Jason Archambault, director of behavioral economics at Truist Financial

"An engaging and thoughtful read packed with tons of concrete examples, this book is a valuable resource for anyone seeking to understand the principles of behavioral science and apply them in their work and lives."

—Bec Weeks, cofounder of Pique

"Like Melina's podcast, *What Your Customer Wants and Can't Tell You* sparkles with snappy ideas that unearth truths about human behavior with cool ideas and practical tips. It stands on the shoulders of her podcast guests and researchers who shared great ideas, but, more importantly, Melina serves them up in ways that are down-to-earth and easy to put into practice. It's a must-read!"

—Tim Houlihan, chief behavioral strategist at Behavior Alchemy and cohost of the award-winning *Behavioral Grooves* podcast

"*What Your Customer Wants and Can't Tell You* is absolutely jam-packed full of fascinating examples of how, deep-down, our brains are shaping, guiding, and triggering everyday behavior…without us even being aware of it! Energizing, fun, and pacy, this book will appeal not just to smart-marketers, creatives, and designers looking for fresh inspiration, but to anybody interested in the latest science behind what really makes us tick… and what it is that nudges us to make the choices we do."

—Thom Noble, president/CSO of CloudArmy Inc.

"*What Your Customer Wants and Can't Tell You* is a stand-out guide for anyone fascinated by customer behavior and the science of decision-making. Melina is an invaluable voice in the field, with a unique take on behavioral economics and its application for marketers. *What Your Customer Wants and Can't Tell You* is accessible in its delivery and robust in its evidence base for enthusiasts and practitioners alike, providing clear examples and memorable insight—a smart balance of breadth and depth."

—Madeline Quinlan, cofounder of Salient Behavioral Consultants and head of membership for the Global Association of Applied Behavioral Scientists

"Any business needs to understand human behavior—and therefore how people think—to succeed. Melina Palmer's brilliant book brings to life the latest science explaining why we do what we do, using engaging and relatable examples, and gives you immediately practical advice and tips on how to apply it for your business. Read it so you—and your business— can benefit."

—Richard Chataway, author of *The Behaviour Business* and CEO of BVA Nudge Unit UK

"This book is a great resource for people wanting to make human behavior work for their business and impact their lives."

—Dr. Marco Palma, director of the Human Behavior Laboratory at Texas A&M University

"Melina has made the complex workings of the human brain, the most powerful machine on the planet even in the Age of AI, simple and approachable for anyone to understand and take advantage of."

—James Robert Lay, founder and CEO of Digital Growth Institute and podcast host and author of *Banking on Digital Growth*

"Melina uses relatable anecdotes and beautifully simple narratives that speak directly to the mind and emotions of the reader. In doing so, she illustrates the point of the book: Why it's fundamental to truly understand human emotions and behavior in a quantifiable way and the tools you need to do so to ultimately connect to customers and demonstrate real growth."

—Nadia Haagen Pedersen, executive vice president of marketing at iMotions

"This book is an incredible, step-by-step guide for people in the business world who want to deepen their understanding of behavioral economics to give themselves a competitive edge in the market. I highly recommend Melina as a go-to expert in the field, and this book is a leading resource for me as I seek to deepen my knowledge in the field."

—Kwame Christian, director of the American Negotiation Institute, bestselling author, attorney, speaker, and host of the number-one negotiation podcast, *Negotiate Anything*

"At its most basic, success in business is a result of understanding human behavior better than your competitors. From that perspective, *What Your Customer Wants and Can't Tell You* is the most important business book to come out in years. Behavioral economist-slash-podcaster-slash-author Melina Palmer provides an all-encompassing guide to navigating the complexities of the human brain to get people to buy from you."

—Michael F. Schein, author of *The Hype Handbook* and president of MicroFame Media

"Einstein said, 'Everything should be made as simple as possible, but not simpler.' *What Your Customer Wants and Can't Tell You* does just that, as Melina Palmer takes a tremendous amount of research from behavioral economics and social psychology and shares it in ways anyone can understand. And she does so without losing the nuances you need to know if you want to get it right. Most importantly, Melina gives real-world applications and additional references for readers who want to dive deeper into the topic. This book, and her Brainy Business podcast, are resources you don't want to overlook if you want to become more persuasive."

—Brian Ahearn, author of *Influence PEOPLE*

"*What Your Customer Wants and Can't Tell You: Unlocking Consumer Brains with the Science of Behavioral Economics* is a fascinating book on human behavior and economics. This thorough guidebook will shape the way you do business and force you to rethink your current strategies. It includes practical exercises to help you move your current management mess to leadership and business success. This is a must-read for anyone who wants to understand their clientele and what makes them tick."

—Scott J. Miller, bestselling author and host of the number-one leadership podcast, *On Leadership with Scott Miller*

"From complete beginners to seasoned professionals, everyone who reads *What Your Customer Wants and Can't Tell You* will glean invaluable nuggets of wisdom about the art of applying behavioral science to business and brands."

—April Vellacott, behavioral consulting lead at Cowry Consulting and coauthor of *Ripple: The BIG Effects of Small Behavior Changes in Business*

"Building on the success of her podcast, Palmer has crafted a thoughtful, approachable book for anyone looking to take their first foray into the world of applied behavioral science and how it can be applied to practical business problems."

—Matt Wallaert, behavioral scientist and author of *Start at the End: How to Build Products that Create Change*

"*What Your Customer Wants and Can't Tell You* is packed full of practical insights and real-world case studies and is fully supported with academic references. A book to devour if you want to get your teeth into the application of behavioral economics."

—Jez Groom, founder and CEO of Cowry Consulting and coauthor of *Ripple: The BIG Effects of Small Behavior Changes in Business*

"With thoughtful application of the concepts from *What Your Customer Wants and Can't Tell You*, you will outsmart the nonconscious barriers that keep you from doing your best work, and in the process, outpace your competition and create products, services, and experiences for your customers that even they don't know how to ask for. Get it, absorb it, use it!"

—Adam Hansen, principal and VP of behavioral innovation at Ideas To Go and coauthor of *Outsmart Your Instincts*

"In *What Your Customer Wants and Can't Tell You*, Melina lifts up the curtain to help us understand what customers often don't understand themselves—how they make decisions. This brilliant book is a wealth of knowledge, arming practitioners with actionable insights to help understand how customers decide."

—Nate Andorsky, CEO of Creative Science and author of *Decoding the Why: How Behavioral Science Is Driving the Next Generation of Product Design*

"Practical advice and engaging exercises to help you start applying behavioral science in your business right away."

—Aline Holzwarth, head of behavioral science at Pattern Health and principal at Duke University's Center for Advanced Hindsight

"If you are already a fan of Melina's excellent podcast *The Brainy Business* (as I am!), you'll instantly recognize her friendly and warm voice in *What Your Customer Wants and Can't Tell You*. Displaying her usual upbeat and enthusiastic style, Melina succeeds in making the subject of behavioral economics seem cool and fun to explore."

—Louise Ward, cohost of the *Behavioural Science Club*

"From the hardest-working podcaster in the field of behavioral science, *What Your Customer Wants and Can't Tell You* is a must-read packed with useful case studies and practical advice for brands and organizations alike."

—Dr. Benny Cheung, director at Dectech

"*What Your Customer Wants and Can't Tell You* hands you the key to the secret world of behavioral science, in its comprehensive yet approachable review of the research and how to use it."

—Patrick Fagan, chief scientific officer of Capuchin Behavioral Science and author of *Hooked: Why Cute Sells and Other Marketing Magic that We Just Can't Resist*

"An eminently readable guide to unconscious persuasion written by an industry veteran—get this book before your competitors do!"

—Tim Ash, international keynote speaker and bestselling author of *Unleash Your Primal Brain*

"Melina does an amazing job of taking such a fascinating, yet complex, topic and distilling it into simple, actionable information that can be applied in so many different aspects of our lives."

—Michael Mazur, VP of Business Development at Colu

"The book every businessperson should read! It's packed full of thoughtful information and laid out in a way that is easy to absorb. It will make you think and act differently, as well as approach your business in a whole new way. It will make you laugh, gasp, and ponder. It's absolutely brilliant."

—Nikki Rausch, CEO of Sales Maven, neurolinguistic programming expert, podcast host, and author of *Buying Signals* and *The Selling Staircase*

WHAT YOUR CUSTOMER WANTS

AND CAN'T TELL YOU

WHAT YOUR CUSTOMER WANTS
AND CAN'T TELL YOU

Unlocking Consumer Brains
with the Science of Behavioral Economics

MELINA PALMER

CORAL GABLES

For permission requests, please contact the publisher at:
Mango Publishing Group
2850 S Douglas Road, 2nd Floor
Coral Gables, FL 33134 USA
info@mango.bz

For special orders, quantity sales, course adoptions and corporate sales, please
email the publisher at sales@mango.bz. For trade and wholesale sales, please
contact Ingram Publisher Services at customer.service@ingramcontent.com or
+1.800.509.4887.

What Your Customer Wants and Can't Tell You: Unlocking Consumer Brains with the
Science of Behavioral Economics

Library of Congress Cataloging-in-Publication number: 2021934472
ISBN: (print) 978-1-64250-562-7, (ebook) 978-1-64250-563-4
BISAC category code PSY031000, PSYCHOLOGY / Social Psychology

Printed in the United States of America

For Aaron, who makes everything possible.

Table of Contents

Foreword

Exactly one hundred years ago, a publisher in London released *The Psychology of Persuasion* by William Macpherson. In 1929, Edward Bernays popularized smoking among women by reframing cigarettes as "torches of freedom." Despite the gradual development of the field of consumer psychology, though, all too many twentieth-century managers doggedly stuck to marketing focused on features and benefits.

Meanwhile, though, entirely new academic disciplines were evolving. Economists who had focused on complex equations to explain the world found that their most basic assumptions about human behavior were wrong. Consumers do not always seek the greatest marginal utility, and managers do not always strive to maximize profits. Behavioral economics became an important field, with multiple Nobel prizes awarded for work showing how humans really act.

In the last few decades, neuroscience has added still more to our knowledge of human behavior. Imaging tools like fMRI turned the brain from an impenetrable black box into something that could be observed in action.

My own interest in the intersection of marketing and the brain grew when I saw that a few forward-thinking marketers were using the tools of neuroscience to study customer reactions to advertising, packaging, and products.

I began writing about the nascent field of neuromarketing in 2005. I became a bit frustrated in those early days, because, at the time, only big brands could afford neuromarketing studies. Because of this, my writing increasingly focused on brain-based marketing tactics that any size organization could use.

During this time, a series of bestselling books showed that most human decisions are made mostly at the nonconscious level. Business leaders became increasingly aware that their customers might not be persuaded by logic and facts alone.

When my first book, *Brainfluence*, came out nearly a decade ago, there were few guides to help businesspeople use the insights of behavioral science to answer everyday questions. How should one set and display prices? Which image will be more persuasive? Which headline will attract more buyers? I strove to answer questions like this in a way that any businessperson could not only understand but put into action.

What Your Customer Wants and Can't Tell You by Melina Palmer is a significant and worthy addition to this genre. She explains the science, not in academic terms, but in a way that busy marketers and executives can understand and internalize. Her style is conversational, not didactic or pedantic, and she avoids academic jargon. Melina includes interactive "Try It Yourself" sections to help the reader apply the knowledge to their own situation.

Any reader who completes *What Your Customer Wants and Can't Tell You* will come away with an understanding of a wide range of nonconscious persuasion techniques applicable to organizations of any size. Even those who dive into a particular section can come away with useful ideas.

Successful marketers must go beyond touting the features of their product or service and focus on the nonconscious factors that drive customer decisions. In *What Your Customer Wants and Can't Tell You*, Melina Palmer shows you how to do exactly that.

Roger Dooley, author of *Friction* and *Brainfluence*

PART I

HOW THE BRAIN (AND THIS BOOK) WORK

CHAPTER 1

Unlocking the Secrets of the Brain

What do you know about your brain?

Take a moment now to consider what it does and how it works. What do you truly "know" for sure? How much of what you believe about your brain is built on assumption and wishful thinking? And, to take it a step further, how much do you know about the brain of your best friend, colleague, or customer?

The truth is, even though we all have brains…we don't really understand how they work.

The past twenty years have uncovered more about the human brain than was learned throughout the preceding 200,000 years.[1] Technology and the combined power of a connected world have contributed to this learning, and there is still so much more to discover in the years to come.

One of the best things (in my opinion, at least) to come out of this time is the field of behavioral economics—the psychology of why people buy and the rules of the brain that help us predict what people will actually do instead of what we think they *should*.

I like to say that, if traditional economics and psychology had a baby, you would have behavioral economics. Or, put another way:

Traditional Economics + Psychology
= Behavioral Economics

And good news! That is the most complex equation you will find in this book. Because, while I am a behavioral economist (and I know the title can be a little intimidating), it is my mission to make the learnings from this field accessible and usable by everyone.

This book will:

- Enlighten you on how the human brain works

- Introduce you to some key concepts from the field of behavioral economics: bite-sized chunks that are easy to digest and retain

- Show how you can then combine and *use* those concepts in your business to be more successful

- Teach you some of the brain tricks that would otherwise keep you stuck, so you can push past them and implement what you learn here

Behavioral economics is a field rooted in science, the result of decades of research from multiple disciplines around the world: psychology, economics, neuroscience, and philosophy, to name a few. However, it is also an art. There are hundreds of rules, concepts, and stimuli working together in the brain to shape your reality and decision-making. The concepts introduced in this book are proven, and we all experience them in some way…but choosing which to apply, as well as when and how to apply them? That's where the art comes in. This book will explain how I approach this in my own work and how you can do the same.

First, let's talk more about how the brain really works.

The Receptionist and the Executive

Let's say you want to have a meeting with Oprah. You can't just call her up and get an appointment on the calendar—you need to make it through a receptionist (or ten) first. The "gatekeeper," who keeps every little thing from making it to the remarkably busy Oprah, is a lot like the relationship between your conscious and subconscious brain.

Nobel Prize-winning behavioral economist Daniel Kahneman talks about the brain in two systems.[2] **System One** (which I will call the "subconscious" throughout this book and *The Brainy Business* podcast) is the automatic system. It is quick to react and can handle an incredible amount of information at any given time—to put it into computer terms, as much as eleven million bits of information per second.[3]

By contrast, **System Two** is what I refer to as your conscious brain. It is much slower and cannot handle nearly as much information. Compared to the subconscious's eleven million bits per second, the conscious brain can only do about forty bits (yikes).

Subconscious (System One) = Receptionist

Uses proven rules to make tons of quick, automatic decisions

Conscious (System Two) = Busy Executive

Only really important stuff makes it to this level; slower, more evaluative decisions

While we like to think we're in control of our brains and all our decisions (and believe we are doing everything as a complex, logical evaluation), it simply isn't the case. The conscious brain cannot handle enough information to get through the plethora of decisions needed to survive.

That is why 99 percent of the decisions you make (as well as those of your customers, colleagues, friends, and family members) are handled by the subconscious brain.[4]

Unfortunately, these two systems of the brain don't speak the same language. That is why focus groups will say they want to buy toothpaste A...and then don't. They aren't lying to you on purpose (for the most part). It turns out people don't know what they will do. And even worse, they can't even tell you after the fact why they *did* something because, again, the two parts of the brain aren't speaking the same language.

Learning the Rules

Think back to when you first learned to drive a car. It was likely a slow, tedious process where you were constantly second-guessing yourself. ("Where do my hands go? Which pedal is that? Don't forget to check the mirror!")

It was slow because your conscious brain was having to learn and set up rules for the process. Now that those rules have been established, it's much easier—you likely didn't even need to think about any of that the last time you drove, right? That's because driving skills have moved into your subconscious brain. While you drive, your brain is still making all the same decisions and evaluations, but they are done quickly using established rules of thumb—things that have worked in the past.

Everything's smooth and easy—until you're driving over a mountain pass in the pouring rain between a semi-truck and a guard rail—then you can feel reality shift and slow...way...down. You're aware of every tiny shift in the wheel against your hands, every eye movement feels intense, your shoulders are raised, and you're hyper-aware.

That is the process of your subconscious handing the wheel over to your conscious brain (pun intended). Driving in this moment is too important and needs diligent focus to keep you safe. It's worthy of those forty bits per second (and something else needs to be relegated down to the level of the subconscious while driving takes precedence).

This is also why you turn the radio down while searching for a new address; the conscious brain can't handle that much input at one time.

While the driving example shows how your brain has created rules and biases based on your individual experiences, the subconscious's rules are also greatly influenced by our biology and have been developing for thousands of years.[5]

Consider the "fight, flight, or freeze" response we all have when confronted by danger. There's a reason our automatic process takes over in those intense situations—it needs to protect us based on what has kept us (and our ancestors) alive for generations. Any of our relatives who saw two reflective dots in the bushes during the night and thought, "Nah, I know you all think that's a tiger…but I bet you're wrong!" probably didn't make it through the evolutionary chain before being eaten by said tiger.

Past Predictions Shape the Future

Both types of learning—those created through the generations and via our individual experiences—influence the rules the subconscious lives by and constantly applies throughout the day.

Almost everything you do in life is based on a prediction of what is coming next, which is based on the subconscious's understanding of the past; it churns through choices and usually does quite well. However, more often than we realize, the subconscious is using rules that don't perfectly fit the situation at hand (as you will see repeatedly through the examples explaining the concepts in Part II). With eleven million bits to process every second, it's no wonder that every single decision isn't 100 percent on point.

For example, most of us aren't in real danger of meeting tigers these days, but the brain still applies our fight, flight, or freeze response when we are "attacked" by a meeting with the boss or overwhelmed by ads on a website.

The most important thing for you to know as you go through this book (and evaluate your life and business decisions moving forward) is that behavioral economics helps us understand these rules of the brain. The concepts I will introduce you to throughout this book have been proven across culture, age, gender, income, education, and more.[6] They may appear in different degrees and are not exactly the same for every person in every situation, but we all do each of these things to varying degrees in our lives every day.

Imagine you were seeing a chess board for the first time and sat down to play against a master, but you weren't allowed to know the rules and had to learn as you went. You might come up with theories and guesses for what each piece could do, or why and when to move one, but it would be incredibly difficult to make progress and you would almost never win.

How much could you learn at each point if you knew the rules going in? How different would that experience be?

To me, understanding behavioral economics and how the brain makes decisions can set you up to be the chess master playing against a fumbling novice. When you have the rules of the game and most of the world doesn't, what sort of leg up can you have in life and business?

Let's find out.

CHAPTER 2

Businesses and Brands

"A brand is a memory."

–PETER STEIDL, PHD, AUTHOR OF *NEUROBRANDING*[7]

What are your favorite brands?

Whatever came to mind for you, the response was essentially instantaneously generated by your subconscious brain. The reaction was likely more than a black-and-white business ledger, but one infused with emotion, memories, and an evocation of the senses. Maybe you saw the Apple logo in your mind, or could almost taste (and instantly crave) your favorite Starbucks Frappuccino, or felt the thrill of your first family trip to Disneyland, or could smell the leather seats in your Volvo.

Your brain's association with those favorite brands has become a subconscious rule and association—a habit. But what goes into establishing them as a *favorite* brand? Why do you relate to them differently than any other business? Why are these the ones that come to mind, and what is it about them that you love so much?

You may have heard the old adage that "perception is reality," and people continue to say that because it's true. In this case, I prefer Peter Steidl's statement that "a brand is a memory."

Unlike a mere business, a *brand* has risen to something more.

A business is the exchange of goods or services for money. Businesses are here to bring in revenue. But what makes someone more likely to want to buy from one business over another? What ties back to the emotion, story, and memory? Branding.

A brand is a collection of experiences that make up a persona in your mind, and familiarity breeds liking.[8]

Imagine you are set up on a blind date. How critical are you of that person's actions? Everything they say and do is being evaluated and tallied. An annoying slurp of the soup could be enough to place this otherwise wonderful person into the reject pile forever.

Now imagine you're married, and your partner makes a similarly annoying soup slurp...is it time to file for divorce?

Probably not.

It's the same thing with brands. When you first meet them, you are on high alert—your defenses are high, and you are ready for them to do something that will allow you to categorize them as a hero or a zero. During this process, your brain is using a combination of subconscious and conscious techniques to evaluate the brand: much of what is happening and influencing your choices is below your level of conscious understanding.

Once they've passed the evaluation phase and transitioned to a known—or even better, a *favorite*—brand, they might "slurp the soup" from time to time and still be a ten.

If they did something really appalling, would that distort the relationship? How many bad experiences would it take for your absolute favorite brand to no longer be at the top of your list? Could they upset you and shake that loyalty to its core? And now that you're thinking about it…why do you really buy from them? Is it loyalty or habit?

From Business to Branding

Brands are important because they are what connects your business to the brain of the customer. The subconscious is emotional and motivated to act (or not) because of what it expects will give it the rewards it craves. Without a brand—without those memories—your business cannot become a habit for the subconscious brain. And if you aren't the habit, your competitors will be.

No matter what you are doing or selling, the brand is at the core. Think of some of those top brands I mentioned earlier—the crème de la crème in business. They know who they are, what they are about, what they are not, and why.

Gibson Biddle, former VP of product at Netflix, says building great products, companies, and brands begins with a shift from customer focus to customer *obsession*.[9] Their behavioral approach allowed them to be ahead of competitors, creating products and services customers didn't know to ask for. It's an advantage you can gain for your own business using the tips in this book.

Disney is a brand of magic, wonder, and living out dreams. Your memories of their brand come with expectations. Could you imagine having the whole family sit down to a movie and having it be a gore-fest like *Saw*?

People would be outraged. It wouldn't take long to ruin their reputation and damage the brand.

Everything they do, from the experience in the stores to the "cast members" at the parks, is part of their brand. Disney knows that every person matters. Every moment matters. And everything needs to be in line with the brand.

The Power of Novelty and Story

Disney isn't the only brand to incorporate such detail into its work. The Venetian Hotel in Las Vegas, which was named the most extraordinarily designed hotel in the world by TripAdvisor in 2014, could have used any marble for its twenty-five-foot-high columns, but chose to have them imported from Italy for authenticity. Amazon could have used plain cardboard boxes, but instead includes its logo (with a smile that suggests how the company ships everything from A to Z). Every advertising image of the iPhone shows it set to 9:41 a.m., which is the time it was first unveiled by Steve Jobs in 2007. Speaking of times in ads, did you know that nearly every advertisement for a watch has the time set at 10:10 a.m.? This is done because of the symmetry and, like the Amazon logo, it's reminiscent of a smiling face. (We will revisit this in the priming chapters in Part II.) The bird in Twitter's logo has a name (it's Larry, in case you're wondering). And all those portraits in the Harry Potter movies? They were hand painted by artists, not computer-generated. (I've seen them on the Warner Bros. set in London, they are fantastic!)

This list could go on and on—it could probably fill its own book. But our question is, *why*?

Why do our favorite brands go to all this trouble? Why not cut corners? Why give Barbie a full name and backstory? (To save you a Google search, it's Barbara Millicent Roberts, and she grew up in [fictional] Willows, Wisconsin.)

One reason is that our brains love the little wins and discoveries. We love to know how thoughtful the company is—it feels like a gift, and the knowledge can help us sound smart at cocktail parties. This can also create a halo effect.[10] The brain thinks, "If they put this much attention into the peripheral stuff, imagine how much they care about the main stuff!"

Another reason is that our brains are perceptive. The processing of those eleven million bits a second the subconscious is dealing with is programmed to pick up on things that are off the mark.

Consider *Game of Thrones*. Seventy-three episodes over eight seasons. Glorious costumes and sets portrayed for more than 252,000 seconds—and then, one rogue Starbucks cup in the final season set the internet on fire.

Why does this stand out like a sore thumb? And why didn't the masses feel the same need to tweet about the millions of items that were properly shown throughout the show? Why will this one slip-up reflect disproportionately negatively upon the entire franchise?

Because of those constant brain scans, which are programmed to alert the conscious mind when something is off. All those other micro-moments throughout the show are just a blur in the background (and, I agree, it isn't fair that people don't write articles about all the little things they got right). The memory will blow that tiny inconsistency way out of proportion, and it will impact all the associated memories too.

A Collection of Memories

Remember, a brand is a collection of memories, bound together to create an impression on the brains that interact with it. Each time your customer interacts with your brand, millions of pieces of information are sorted and filed by the subconscious brain, and their perception of your business is constantly evolving with each new experience.[11]

But what are memories and how do they work?

A seemingly simple question with a complex answer—and one full of truths many of us would prefer to ignore. When you think about your brain and its memories, you may relate it to a filing cabinet, or possibly think about it like a photo being stored in the cloud. We like to think that each memory is an exact copy of what happened, in all its intricate detail, stored in a secure place to look at whenever we want and then put back in the exact same condition it was in when we took it out.

Unfortunately, that's completely wrong.

Our memories are basically inaccurate renditions our brains tell us, and every time we access them, we change them a little. So, the more you think about something…the less and less it's like the original version. Frustrating, right?

Every person's brain is constantly changing their memories to better suit their own needs: making themselves look better, exaggerating certain parts and playing down the importance of others, all without our conscious knowledge. It can even create false memories: where someone believes something happened to them, even though it was only in a story or advertisement.[12]

At eighteen, I started working in an airline call center and quickly made my way into the Customer Care Department. You know all those times you were annoyed at the airline and called to yell at someone? That was me.

It was amazing to hear the stories some people would tell about their experiences. The horror of the most terrible flight delay: "It was *excruciating!*" they would say, "I was stranded at the airport with no food and uncomfortable seating and the bathroom was a mess…"

A few clicks in the computer and, come to find, their flight was delayed for ninety minutes.

In case you didn't know, every single person who calls to complain to an airline will ask for a free ticket. I once had a woman ask for a free ticket because the flight attendants took too long to give her a can of soda on the flight (she was in row eight).

Perception is reality in these memories, and the experiences people have while stuck in the airport for a lightning storm will impact the airline's brand even though the weather is beyond their control. Logically, people know the airline is making choices to keep everyone safe. But the subconscious brain isn't keeping that in mind when it files the experience away as a memory.

Think about the old fishing-tale example, where someone caught a minnow and twenty years later it was "a whopper—the biggest thing you've ever seen!" They are not intentionally lying (usually). In their brain, the fish actually gets bigger each time they tell the story, as they unknowingly level out some facts to exaggerate others. This is a natural tendency of the brain, and we do this in all sorts of experiences…not just to look good to other fishermen.[13]

Another funny quirk, which is particularly important for companies to know, is that the brain doesn't always know the difference between what actually happened to us and something we *think* happened.

Do you remember that time you got lost in the mall when you were five years old? You were walking with your mom and a fluffy orange teddy bear caught your eye. It was fascinating, because orange isn't a common color for a bear, and it looked so cuddly through the glass. In what felt like a second, you looked back, and your mom's black-and-white-striped dress was nowhere to be found. Fear surged within you as you started to panic and look frantically around at the legs of adults quickly walking by. They say it was only twelve minutes before you and Mom were reunited, but it felt like a lifetime.

Believe it or not, your brain has now stored this little tidbit in your memory banks. Even though it is a fake memory, your brain doesn't always file it that way. In one famous study,[14] a third of people who were reminded of "that time they were lost in the mall" (which never happened) believed it to be true. One-quarter continued to claim the untrue story as a real memory after two follow-up interviews.

And the more something is said, the more we believe it.[15]

Advertising claims, like "best in class," "the greatest network coverage," or "fastest-growing company," are all stored as truths in the memory banks of customers. And our brains like consistency, so once we have heard that thing, we believe it to be true, and look for things that confirm that expectation.[16]

Hindsight may seem to be 20/20, but those memories are not always what they appear.

Should Is a Four-Letter Word

If you are creating a product or service that people "should" want and they don't buy it…is it really worth selling?

Here at The Brainy Business, "should" is a four-letter word. If you have ever found yourself saying "people *should* buy this" or "anyone *should* be able to figure out this is a great deal," it's time to stop and reflect.

People do not always do what they "should" or what is in their best interest. Even if they *know* what is best, it doesn't mean they will do that thing. We all want to be healthier, and we know what it takes to reach that very achievable dream: diet and exercise.

But do we do what we know we *should*? More often than not…no.

This is the conundrum of the brain: the conscious "knows" what to do but can't get the subconscious to follow orders. NYU psychologist Jonathan Haidt[17] explains this with a fantastic example of someone riding an elephant.

The rider (conscious brain, System Two) can have the best plan and all the logic in the world, but if the elephant (subconscious brain, System One) is distracted or uninterested…it will win without needing to consult the rider. Pushing or pulling the elephant, yelling at it, or pouting won't get it to move. But the right nudge of encouragement—perhaps a pool of cool water on a hot day?—and look out, subconscious is on a mission!

Working with the brain—helping the rider and the elephant to be on the same path—is always easier than trying to pull the elephant along. That is where The Brainy Business's approach to behavioral economics steps in.

This book will help you unlock the brain and its concepts; you will understand how these concepts can be combined and applied in all sorts of ways to give you a leg up in business.

The biggest problem for businesses—whether you are designing the product, setting price points, creating the marketing messages, communicating internally among staff, or developing a cohesive brand— is that the conscious "rider" is trying to talk to other riders in their own language when they should actually be working to entice the elephant first.

Elephants don't understand human logic, and the subconscious brain is the same way. Start with the elephant, and the rider will help explain why it was a fantastic idea.

CHAPTER 3

Important Brain Stuff

The subconscious "elephant" is constantly searching for rewards and likes knowing where to find them (which is why it prefers the status quo, where it has a solid path to getting them whenever it wants). There are four main "feel-good" brain chemicals that keep us coming back for more, which you can remember by the acronym DOSE:[18]

- Dopamine: anticipation

- Oxytocin: empathy and social bonding

- Serotonin: mood (good or bad)

- Endorphins: masking pain or discomfort (important in reaching goals)

Dopamine and Anticipation

While all these chemicals matter, in my opinion, dopamine is most relevant for most business purposes. Habits, which drive 95 percent of buying behavior, are built on the anticipation of a reward.[19] And while it may feel like the benefit is in the treat itself, the journey really matters most.

A study by neuroscientist Robert Sapolsky[20] was looking to see when dopamine was released in the reward process, and started by training monkeys to know that, when a light went on, if they pressed a button ten times, they would receive a treat.

When do you think the dopamine release *begins* and when is it *highest*?

- When the light goes on

- While pressing the button

- When the treat is released

- When consuming the treat

For any of us who have consumed treats of our own, we might think the best part is when we get and consume it.

Here's what really happens: the dopamine release *begins* when the light comes on, and it is at its *highest* while pushing the button. It ends when the treat is released.

The crazy part is how uncertainty changes things. Making it so the treats were only released 50 percent of the time *doubled* the dopamine released! And when the rules changed so treats were delivered either 25 percent or 75 percent of the time, they had the same level of release—about halfway between getting a reward half the time and every time.

UNCERTAINTY INCREASES DOPAMINE

The joy of an experience comes from the anticipation of the reward, not the reward itself.

Think about that as you build out your programs and customer experience journeys: It really is all about the journey.

There are several chapters dedicated to that process throughout the book. As you'll see, expectations determine dopamine levels, and negative dopamine is terrible for brands. If you hype up an experience with a lot of anticipation and the delivery falls short? You get negative dopamine and angry customers. In reverse, when delivery exceeds the expectations and anticipation levels, there is extra dopamine (i.e. surprised and delighted customers, which has its own chapter in Part II).

Think about using a vending machine to get a snack. You expect to pay for one thing and then to receive it. Not a lot of dopamine released. Have you ever gotten a *bonus* item when two treats fell for the price of one? Woo! Extra dopamine. What about when you pay and it gets stuck, so your treat doesn't fall? Boo! Negative dopamine.

The gift of a free sample for something people might be hesitant about trying (but that you know is amazing) is a great double whammy of reciprocity and the dopamine released with anticipation.

Mirror Neurons

Another important thing to know about our brains is the amazing way we learn and empathize with others: mirror neurons.[21] Scientists have, of course, long known we learn by observation and have empathy for others we may have never met before, but they didn't really know why until mirror neurons were discovered in the early 1990s.

Let me tell you a story…

Once upon a time, on a particularly hot day, there was a monkey in a lab at the University of Parma in Italy. It had some electrodes placed to test motor control and determine which areas of the brain would light up when it grabbed a cup (or a peanut) to drink water (or eat said peanut). This would allow the scientists to understand how the brain reacts in various motor control actions, and if reactions were different when the monkey grabbed a cup, a block, or a peanut.

On this fateful day, one of the researchers reportedly came in eating an ice cream cone. The monkey didn't move. From the outside, all someone might have noticed was the monkey's eyes widening with interest, but the brain told a different story. The monkey's brain lit up as if it was eating the ice cream itself!

Further studies found that when a person grabbed the peanut to hand it to the monkey, its brain would light up *as if it were grasping the peanut itself*. And if a researcher put a peanut in their own mouth…the monkey's brain would light up as if it were eating a peanut as well! Even when no movement occurs, the brain "experiences" tasks being done by others as if it were experiencing these same things itself.

This allowed the team to accidentally discover mirror neurons, and related studies were first published in the 1990s.[22] Like monkeys, we humans have mirror neurons as well, and they have shaped our existence.

Mirror neurons help us learn by observation:

- A child watching an adult open a jar can learn how to open a jar when presented with one.

- A ballerina being taught a proper *pas de chat* can also learn by observation.

- Aspiring public speakers can watch others give presentations and get tips for what to do (and not to do) themselves.

All this can be done without talking to anyone or physically performing the acts, which is astonishing when you think about it. And without mirror neurons, life as we know it would not exist. (What would YouTube do without all those unboxing videos?)

The first human to discover fire presumably did so by accident. I highly doubt they had a process of trial and error working toward achieving this goal of heat and fire. So, how did all the other humans learn quickly to replicate and do this thing themselves?

That's right, mirror neurons.

This is also how the species learned to hunt, gather, farm, build homes, and all the skills we use every day. The collective intelligence of the species grows very quickly as one person learns to do something because others can watch and have their brains behave as if they have already done it once before. These learnings spread like wildfire (pun very much intended).

Let's revisit how mirror neurons work. We each have 100 billion neurons in our brains, and each of those neurons has one thousand to ten thousand contacts with other neurons, forming associations.

Mirror neurons are found in the frontal lobes. The front of the brain is also home to our ordinary motor control neurons, which fire when performing a specific action (grab a cup, kick a ball—things like that). Mirror neurons fire when we experience these actions, but not for meaningless gestures.

Even more amazing, and important in your brand execution, is that *intention* matters. In one study, participants were shown a hand picking up a teacup in three different scenarios:[23]

- with a plate of cookies and pot of tea nearby (to simulate picking up to take a sip)

- amidst crumbs and a messy table (to simulate cleaning up)

- no context (hand and teacup against a blank background)

The mirror neurons were more active when the context was included: they respond best to actions with clear goals.

They also help us understand the actions of others and empathize with them. For example, when you see someone else being touched on the right forearm—by another person, or with an object like a feather duster— your brain reacts as if you are being touched on your right forearm in the same way.

As Vilayanur Ramachandran explains in his great TED talk, your brain's pain and touch receptors are smart enough to tell your brain, "Don't worry, no one is touching us, we're just empathizing," which keeps you from consciously experiencing it. And even if you received an injection so your arm was numb, you would still experience and "feel" the touch!

Amazing, but true. And it's all thanks to mirror neurons.

This is fascinating, yes. But you may be wondering, "Why does this matter in a book about applying behavioral economics in business?" Here are a few of the limitless applications:

- Videos that let someone see the buying process will make it easier for them to buy

- Taking an extra second at the end of a YouTube video to show a cursor clicking on a "Subscribe" button will greatly increase followers

- The wrong facial expression in an image on your website can trigger the wrong mirror neurons and actions

- Brand stories trigger mirror neurons, so we experience and catalog them differently

- Context is important when driving behavior (remember the teacup)

- Customer relationships are a vicious or virtuous cycle: if you put out negative content, they will be more negative; if you pull out positive content, they will be more positive[24]

Word choice, brand persona, and the attitudes of your staff all matter in the way your company is perceived and how others interact with you. Even if they don't realize it and can't articulate it on a survey, it is impacting their interpretation of you and your business. You'll see that "everything matters" is a consistent theme throughout this book. Whether or not you think about the implications of a choice, they still impact the behavior of your employees, coworkers, and customers. It is your opportunity to shape that experience to be the best one possible and my question is, why wouldn't you?

Biased Brains

Before we jump into the concepts, it is important to acknowledge the biases that exist in our brains. People often aspire to have a completely unbiased perspective. When it comes to the human brain, it is important to know that none of us can be without bias. Ever.

The subconscious brain's rules of thumb are based on past experiences and biases. They are always there. While you can't eliminate them, understanding them can help make everything smoother. One thing our brain's biases do is to make each person believe they are better, smarter, and faster than everyone else.[25]

> *"Everyone thinks they have good taste*
> *and a sense of humor, but they couldn't*
> *possibly all have good taste."*
>
> –CARRIE FISHER AS MARIE, *WHEN HARRY MET SALLY*

Our brains really are the center of their own universe, wired to believe in our own awesomeness. As you think about the following things your brain is doing constantly, remember that these are all the same for your coworkers, family members, customers, leads, and your past self—we all think we are better today than we were yesterday. Our brains are wired to believe:[26]

- Unlike other people, I see reality exactly as it is; I am objective and unbiased (naïve realism)

- I am better than others and more likely to succeed (optimism bias)

- Most people agree with me—silence equals agreement, right? (false consensus effect)

- I understand others better than they understand me (illusion of asymmetric insight)

- I am transparent; everyone should know my motives and backstory without explanation (illusion of transparency)

- I am different from everyone else, I need a custom solution (false uniqueness bias)

- *But*...I see myself in very general situations and say, "That is so me!" to things like horoscopes (Forer effect, Barnum effect, astrology effect, fortune-telling phenomenon)

- If I don't wear my lucky socks, the team will lose (illusion of control)

- I can resist temptation better than everyone else; bring on the timeshare presentation! (optimism bias, overconfidence effect)

- Everyone else is so predictable, but I'm much more dynamic (trait ascription bias)

- I would totally crush on that game show (overconfidence effect)

- That was such a smart choice, I knew it all along (choice supportive bias, illusion of validity)

Behavioral economics shows us that, while we are not identical, we are predictable. It is also important to know that, just because you don't see all the facets of someone else, you are not a three-dimensional creature walking around in a two-dimensional world. And, of course, if you knew that others saw you as two-dimensional compared to them, how might it change the conversation?

CHAPTER 4

How to Use This Book

This book was created to help anyone who is responsible for brand creation and alignment in business to be more effective in that space. Whether you are a CMO of a global corporation, someone in charge of product development and design, head of pricing strategy, or the owner of a small business who wears all these hats—this book is for you.

If you are ready to bring your business savvy to the next level, you're in the right place. This book will help you turn your interest in psychology and the brain and your natural curiosity into bottom-line benefits.

As you go through this book, if you already have a product or service you want help working on, great! Keep that in mind as you go, but don't feel tethered to those "problems" you are thinking of on the way in. The goal of this book is to help you find previously hidden opportunities.

This book was carefully curated into four parts, which are intentionally presented in a specific order:

1. **Part I** was to help you see your brain differently—to know how it really works and be open to learning.

2. **Part II** is dedicated to the concepts that are most applicable in business. They were selected among well over a hundred to give a foundation without being overwhelming. These chapters are short and set up to be a reference of sorts. This book is not meant to sit on a shelf. It was created to be actively used when applying behavioral

economics in your business, so being able to find the concepts easily is important. The end of each chapter includes a prompt or activity for you to start applying the concept on your own, in the same way I do with my clients. And, because there is always more to say and learn, there is a little information about corresponding episodes of *The Brainy Business* podcast if you want to dig deeper on any particular concept. Note: there is a free expanded PDF workbook waiting for you at *thebrainybusiness.com/ApplyIt* so you can take notes and practice again and again.

3. **Part III** builds upon the foundations (concepts) from the previous section and shows how they can be combined in various ways to get incredible results for businesses. Each chapter ends with a list of the concepts, so you may easily reference them as you begin the application process using the prompts provided. (Again, use that free PDF workbook as you go to really reinforce what you learn.)

4. **Part IV** is what helps this book be more than an interesting read. It will share some of your brain's biases and tricks that are there to keep you feeling safe. This will give you the tools and confidence to apply what you learn here in your business without getting stuck.

Before we jump into the concepts, there are a few primers (which will be revisited in Part IV) to get your brain ready for application. Why bring it up in both spots? A few reasons:

1. As you will learn in the chapter on priming, it is important to properly set the stage for your brain. Giving you a hint of the final application will help you think about it as you go, increasing the likelihood of success.

2. Ideally, you will be so excited about the stuff you learn in this book that you can't wait to share some of it before you get all the way to the end. Knowing how to ensure those are productive conversations from the get-go is important to keeping that enthusiasm high (also increasing the likelihood of success).

3. Because of familiarity bias, you will be more receptive to the tips
    at the end when they are presented to you again (you know...to
    increase the likelihood of your success).

So, with your success in mind, here we go with these last few thoughts
before jumping into the concepts.

Challenging the Status Quo

Because our subconscious brains are lazy, they rely on their rules of thumb
(those in this chapter and the concepts throughout the book) to make
decisions. If you let it, your brain would put more and more on autopilot,
enjoying the status quo and fighting everything that threatened that
predictability.[27]

But you are a learner—someone who aspires to grow, change, and
challenge the status quo.

Behavioral economics will become the status quo soon enough. After all,
Bloomberg named "behavioral scientist" the top job of this decade,[28] but,
for now, having these conversations with your company—convincing them
to try these concepts—could go against their own brain biases.

Here are my three tips to help overcome these biased-brain blocks:

1. Help everyone see how they are on the same team, shifting the
    personal biases to include the group (using in-group bias to
    your benefit)

2. Give background information (perhaps from this book) to show
    how we are all similar, and that even when we disagree, we can
    all be right

3. Leverage the power of questions to open the dialogue

How We Can All Be Right

Think back to those eleven million bits of information per second the subconscious can process, compared to the mere forty bits of the conscious brain. When conflicts arise, consider this: for every single piece of information that made it through the filter to your conscious brain, your subconscious essentially marked 275,000 other things as not important or relevant enough.

Isn't it possible that *their* brain filter chose one of the other 275,000 things?

When you approach problems as a chance to think differently—and know that, even when you disagree, you might both be right—it makes it possible to find more interesting solutions and opportunities (both in quality and quantity). As Rory Sutherland says in *Alchemy*,[29] "the opposite of a good idea can still be a good idea."

Leverage the Power of Questions

All my clients have heard me say at least once, "It is easy to find the right answer to the wrong question."

Think of a project in your business—big, small, recent, or old. How long did you spend thinking about the problem before you jumped right into problem-solving mode? (Be honest.)

Think back on all those brain biases outlined earlier. If you are wired to think you understand people better than you do, are more intuitive and perceptive than you really are, are less biased and more capable of solving problems…is it possible that you are jumping into answers before you know the true issue that needs to be addressed?

For some context, Einstein is credited with saying that, if given an hour to solve a problem, he would spend the first fifty-five minutes thinking about the problem and only five working on the solution.

I'm guessing your ratio of problem definition to problem-solving isn't anywhere near that. Are you even spending five minutes of your respective hour identifying the issue?

One of the biggest culprits contributing to the solving-problems-too-soon conundrum is brainstorming. It is built completely backward from what we need to do and is not conducive to the way our brain works. Clients often come to me with questions like, "How can we create the perfect buying experience?" or "How do we get people to choose us instead of our competitors?"

Brainstorming would then force a group of people to throw out possible solutions to the "problem." But, as no one wants to go against the herd, look stupid for throwing out an answer that might be proven wrong, or get saddled with yet *another* project if they share…many good ideas never leave the brain.

The better approach (which I take with my clients) is called questionstorming. It was created by the Right Question Institute,[30] and I first learned about it in my absolute favorite book, *A More Beautiful Question*, by Warren Berger.[31]

We won't get into the whole process here, but I want you to see how questions can open up your mind to opportunity and possibility. Instead of starting with an assumed problem like, "How can we create the perfect buying experience?" and generating lots of solutions, questionstorming begins with a curiosity toward the real problem.

If we turn that into a statement, like, "There is a perfect buying experience," we can now attack that assumption with questions:

- What is perfect?

- Perfect for whom?

- What is the buying experience?

- Does perfection shift from one experience to the next?

- Do people actually want or need "perfect"?

And on and on. In less than half an hour of me leading them through this exercise, teams will regularly generate well over a hundred questions to reflect upon. This creates a better project scope—what matters now and what is not part of the project—so everyone feels comfortable with the direction.

You know the problem and can then work on solving it. And, even though it has been conditioned out of us, our brains are natural questioners. If you doubt me, I've got a four-year-old to send over to your house for an hour or two.

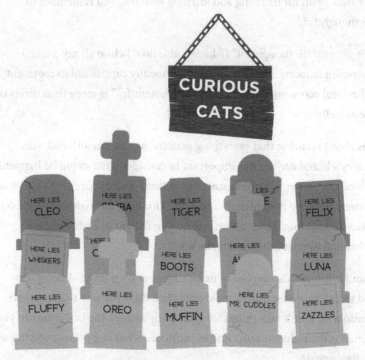

Curiosity killed the cat...or did it?

Curiosity doesn't kill cats.

Did you know there is a second part to that common quote that we conveniently forgot? It became more of a warning against asking questions and learning in its single-line form, but the full quote is actually: "Curiosity killed the cat, satisfaction brought it back."[32]

Properly applied curiosity can reinvigorate and change the course of events. Get curious. Challenge your brain's affinity for the status quo and biases about how things work. Be open to learning what is really going on in your own subconscious so you can understand others better. This simple shift will help you communicate better with coworkers, customers, and anyone else.

Every episode of *The Brainy Business* podcast ends with me saying, "Thanks again for listening and learning with me, and remember to BE thoughtful."

The phrase "BE thoughtful" (which is also how I close all my emails) has multiple facets. First, the BE is intentionally capitalized to represent behavioral economics. The concept of "thoughtful" is more than meets the eye as well.

It is about realizing that everything matters; just as I mentioned with Disney's brand earlier, it is important to consider what might be happening behind the scenes. It's about stopping to think and dig deeper to find more answers than are immediately apparent. Thinking through what someone's subconscious might pick up on and how to delight it, endearing the individual to your brand along the way.

Thoughtfulness also applies to unlocking your own brain. Asking why and wondering how things could apply in a different way than you ever considered. Don't take things for granted or assume the first problem you named is the right (or only) one to consider. What else is there waiting to be discovered?

Give each section the time it needs to be thoughtfully considered. Maybe you go through it all once and then revisit, maybe you pace yourself. However you choose to go through this book, it is the right way for you right now.

Are you ready to change your life and business with behavioral economics? Then let's get started.

Don't forget to download your free PDF workbook with expanded prompts and activities, waiting for you at *thebrainybusiness.com/ApplyIt.*

PART II

CONCEPTS

CHAPTER 5

Framing

Tonight is spaghetti night. Realizing there's no meat for the sauce, you quickly run to the store. They have two stacks of ground beef, side by side:

Which type of ground beef is more appealing?

Which one do you choose?

If you are like most people in the world, you would choose a package from the 90-percent-fat-free stack. But why? Any logical person (or quick reflection) would realize, "That is saying the same thing!"

Even if the 10-percent-fat option was less expensive, it might be hard to convince your brain to buy it, because it sounds so much worse to the subconscious brain.

Do people buy the best thing no matter what? Of course not! Our brains trick us into thinking something is a better option or deal based on the way they hear the information. And while there are ways to get into your conscious space—when forced—it doesn't really work that way in practice.

If you were to take a beautiful painting and put it in a terrible frame, how would that impact your experience and ability to enjoy the artwork itself? What if you took a child's artwork and framed it beautifully?

Why does a little border around the edge make a difference?

It is because the subconscious brain is evaluating everything very quickly and using assumptions to make decisions (like it does with everything else). A high-quality frame or well-placed aesthetic details mean it must be a higher-quality piece.

Similarly, our brains do this all the time with the way words, phrases, or numbers are presented. *What you say is not as important as how you say it.*

When my husband and I moved away from Seattle in 2017, one important task for me was to find a new nail salon. The same location kept being recommended by his coworkers, but it took a while before I could bring myself to go in. Why?

The front of their building had a giant yellow sign that read, "Voted best in the South Sound—2009, 2010, 2011."

The problem with this outdated sign is that it sends a negative message to the subconscious brain. Even if you don't realize it on a conscious level, seeing this message in 2017 doesn't make you think "Wow! They must be great." You think, "Wow, I wonder what happened to make them go downhill these last six years."

The reason for this ending in 2011 could be legitimate—maybe the outlet doing the rankings doesn't make those lists anymore. You still have the accomplishment, so you should be able to tout it. However, you need a new sign, once this gets past a certain point, to keep it from getting stale and becoming a negative.

Instead of listing the specific years, simply say, "Voted best in the South Sound *three years in a row*."

A tiny shift, but that new frame makes all the difference. Three years in a row could have been any time—it could have been forty years ago for all we know, but it doesn't matter. The subconscious brain doesn't read into it that much. It sees the accomplishment for what it is, and the timing becomes a nonissue.

One thing that does matter is *context*. Let's say Steve and Sally each have five million dollars in their bank accounts today. If you were marketing to them, you can consider them as part of the same segment and their messaging can be the same, right?[33]

What if I told you that, yesterday, Steve had one million and Sally had ten million? Would that change things at all?

Do they have a different mindset around the five million dollars in their accounts? Steve is likely ecstatic at his good fortune and Sally is distraught over her loss (more on loss aversion in Chapter 9). The *frames* of their stories and experiences shape the world they each live in. Whenever you are determining the best frame for a message, it is important to consider and understand as much of the context as you can.

Words Matter

Once, on a trip, my husband and I walked past a daycare center called "AVG DAY CARE," as in…*average* daycare. As in mediocre. As in, "Meh…we are just okay."

My question is, why oh why would you do this?

This creates an entire frame around your business that you cannot undo. People will never want to pay you more. People will assume you are middle-of-the-road—you don't put in the extra effort. Who wants that from the place watching and teaching their children? Even if they are trying to be funny, it's not a good approach.

Let's say I decide to open a daycare next door. I am going to call my facility, "Best Daycare Ever" or "A+ Daycare" or "Little Geniuses Daycare" or "Better Than Average Daycare"—truthfully, almost *anything* I choose will be better than the name they have, as I have a better frame.

Putting my company with the better frame next to their poorly framed business will help boost my sales (see Relativity, Chapter 8). Their bad name choice will help me get more business. They might have more experience and lower rates, but it doesn't matter. That poor choice of framing (via a bad name decision) will negatively impact their business for as long as they have it. If you have a name like that, or know someone who does, I urge you to make a change (and tell them to do the same).

Home listings are masterful at choosing words to frame something that could be seen as a negative to feel like a good thing.[34] "Cozy" feels much better to our brains than "small." "Charming" is much more inviting than "old."

"Must see the inside of this cozy, charming home with plenty of usable land for anyone interested in country living."

Sounds much better and different than, "Yes, the outside of this house (which is too far from anywhere to drive to work) is super ugly…and it is quite small and really old, with no privacy, since there are no trees on the property." (Learn more about this in Chapter 6 on Priming.)

In many ways, all the adjectives included in a description could be considered the frame. When something is described as "all-natural," "organic," or "farm-fresh," you assume it is better. The question is, does that truly mean or say anything, or is it just their name or tagline?

Consider Simply Orange. Lovely commercials narrated by Donald Sutherland explain that the product contains nothing but oranges, that the juice is never from concentrate. What about other juices in the bottles next to them? They might use the exact same process, but you don't know for sure. You assume Simply Orange puts in more care than Tropicana or the store brand, but they might not. If you tout something you do—even if everyone else does it too—the implication to the customer's brain is that you are the best at whatever that thing is.

This is a frame—and once someone makes a claim (even if it is something every single one of their competitors could make), it becomes theirs. Everyone else is second in line, and if they try to say it, they will either make themselves look silly, or remind people of the brand that was there first.

The Power of Numbers

If you look around, you can see numbers in almost every advertisement out there—"four out of five dentists agree" or "kills 99.9 percent of germs" or "95 percent would recommend to a friend" or "87 percent of women saw results in six weeks and 99 percent saw results in six months."

Once you start looking for them, you will see numbers everywhere. Gas mileage on the highway versus in town. Percentage of fat or fat-free. 100 percent whole grain. Freshens breath three times better. Twice the cleaning power...I think you get the idea.

Why have you not really noticed the sheer volume of them before? It's because your subconscious brain can easily make a choice when given these number frames. Numbers help your brain value things and make comparisons; they help it decide without flagging your conscious brain. Remember, 99 percent of decisions are made subconsciously. You either make it easy on the brain so it can go with the flow, or you make it hard and induce a shift into the conscious space...which is slow and more likely to get quickly overwhelmed.

Your first step is to look for numbers in your business. You have them. Then, find as many ways as you can to talk about them and see which ones are most compelling.

Once I recommended a client look for a stat like, "87 percent of our customers renew their contracts."

After digging around in the data, she showed me the final stat they wanted to put on the website and other materials: "78 percent of customers get additional services."

While the format is the same as the original recommendation I provided, it doesn't *feel* the same. So, I recommended a change of frame. We shifted it to "four out of five customers get additional services." Doesn't that just *feel* better?

You might be wondering why I recommended the percentage for one and "out of" for the other. Here's why:

87 is a high percentage—it would round up to 90 easily (which in some contexts is basically 100). The brain sees it as high, but 78 percent would only round up to 80—which sounds much lower. And, considering our history with grades, 78 percent is a C and possibly close to failing, depending on your school. It just has negative connotations in the brain. You could also present the number as eight out of ten, but with any fraction, you want to round down to the lowest possible denominator— which leaves you with four out of five, which sounds much better than 78 percent, or even 80 percent, even though it is exactly the same thing.

These all say the same thing, so why do they feel different?

78 percent buy from us again

Eight out of ten buy from us again

Four out of five buy from us again

Most buy from us again

One out of five never come back

Framing Matters.

There are many ways to present information in your business, and you don't have to stay within the strict realm of numbers: "over half" sounds better than 51 percent, and "most" sounds better than 60 percent.

And remember, frames go both ways. Consider the negative flip of each statement (because, even though the subconscious might ignore it, it helps to look at your information from all angles). For example, saying 87 percent of women saw results means 13 percent *didn't*.

Using Jargon Is Bad Framing

Another client, a financial institution, was very excited about their new checking account. They came to me to help with their messaging and planned to have all their billboards with the headline of, "Earn 1.26 percent APY on up to $25,000 in balances."

For most people (even those who love numbers), the brain will gloss over that message and not really pick up on what is being said—especially when driving by at sixty m.p.h. So I recommended they flip the frame and shift the message. The campaign went live with the line, "Did your checking account pay you $315 last year?" and they enjoyed 60 percent month-over-month growth in checking accounts.[35]

Of course, if you do the math of 1.26 percent APY on $25,000, you get $315, but your brain doesn't do the calculation that easily. The lazy subconscious says, "maybe later," and isn't interested enough to move forward.

Take the time to look at all the possible frames for your message before choosing one—don't just go with the first statistic exactly the way you found it.

Applying Framing

Remember: How you say something matters much more than what you are saying.

Try It Yourself: Find a number in your business and look at all the different ways to present it. Try decimals, percentages, fractions, and verbal expressions. Flip each to see what the opposite feels like. Which frame sounds the best? Which ones sound terrible? Does your customer's frame of reference influence the way they would interpret the numbers in any given presentation?

Don't have a number offhand? Practice with this: 256 of 300 people surveyed would recommend you to a friend or family member. Write this data point as a:

Positive Percentage: _____

Negative Percentage: _____

Positive Fraction: _____

Negative Fraction: _____

Positive Verbal Expression: _____

Negative Verbal Expression: _____

Anything Else: _____

More Framing

Find framing again in these chapters: Behavioral Baking (21), The Truth About Pricing (22), How to Sell More of the Right Stuff (23), A Series of Small Steps (24), What Problem Are You Solving? (26)

In my opinion, framing is one of the most important concepts in applied behavioral economics (which is why it kicked off Part II and makes so many appearances in Part III!). It pops up frequently throughout *The Brainy Business* podcast and has two dedicated episodes:

- **(Episode 16) Framing: How You Say Things Matters More Than What You're Saying.** This episode takes a deeper dive into what framing is, and how it can be used in business.

- **(Episode 17) Unlocking the Power of Numbers.** Ever wondered if you should end your pricing in a 5, 7, 9 or 0? This episode explains what matters, how to choose, and why!

CHAPTER 6

Priming

I find that experiencing a concept is the best way to understand (and eventually use) it. To kick this one off, consider the poem below:

> Behavioral economics concepts get shared the most,
> on *The Brainy Business* podcast (where I am host).
> Listen in the car as you drive to the coast.
> Learn lots of new concepts; across social media you'll post.
> Say, what do you put in a toaster?

I am guessing you have seen a trick like this before—you may have even thought, "You won't fool me! I know you want me to say *toast*, but the true answer is *bread*" (or bagels or whatever).

Here's the thing: you know on a *conscious* level that the right answer is bread, but you still need to remind yourself "don't say toast" because your subconscious brain has been primed to give the rhyming answer. Your conscious brain *knows* it's wrong, and you may have stopped yourself from saying "toast" aloud…but you could not stop your brain from thinking "toast" as its first, automatic response.

The human brain is constantly primed by more than just rhymes. Primes can be images, words, smells, sounds, numbers (see Anchoring, Chapter 7), and more. Here are some examples in each category to help you see just how susceptible our brains really are.

Visual Primes

Pick a point on the wall or out the window—or stare at a word on this page—for five seconds.

What if I told you that, while you diligently focused on that single point, your eyes scanned the world around you about fifteen times?

We don't realize it, but our eyes are moving constantly (three times per second on average) and checking the environment for threats.[36] If nothing of note is going on, no alert is sent to your conscious brain because it doesn't need to know, but that doesn't mean the information coming in isn't impacting your behavior.

This is why priming works. And why all those people who say they "never pay attention to ads on social media" or "don't watch commercials" are flat wrong.

Imagine you're sitting in a waiting room, flipping through a magazine until they call your name. You don't realize it, but that magazine included some fake advertisements for made-up companies mixed among the pages. During your time in the following study, you are more likely to recognize or choose that fake brand (whose ad you don't remember seeing) than those who didn't have the modified magazines.[37]

The brain is absorbing and evaluating all that peripheral stuff even if it doesn't hit the consciousness. But when the brain wants a distraction? Or something enticing pops up? Then you notice.

Do you have a special time on the clock where you feel like you always look up and notice it's that time again? For many people it's 11:11 or maybe 12:34 or 5:55. Have you ever wondered why you happen to look up at that exact perfect moment? It may feel like a sign of some higher meaning, but in actuality your eyes noticed the clock hundreds or thousands of other times on those constant eye scans and the subconscious ignored them. No other random time mattered enough to flag the conscious brain. It's also why you buy a green car and start seeing them everywhere. The green cars were always there; your subconscious evaluated and responded using its rules, which didn't generate any reason to waste any of the conscious brain's forty bits on them (until it learned that green cars or a specific time on the clock were important).

Sight happens in the eyes, but vision happens in the brain.

If our eyes are constantly scanning the world around us, why do we not see big blurry blobs all the time? Because, while our sense of sight (which accounts for 70 percent of our body's sense receptors)[38] is taking place in the eyes, vision occurs in the brain.[39]

We have evolved so we can focus on something *and* constantly scan our environment for threats or potential stimuli through saccades. Saccades are why things like flip books work—our brain weaves together a stream of basically still images and connects the missing pieces to create a steady flow of movement. It predicts what is missing to make it look and feel as if it is constant. Cool, right?

This is also why we prefer the status quo: the brain's job is to keep you safe and evaluate as much as possible with existing rules. Predictability and efficiency go hand in hand. And even when you (or your customers) don't consciously notice an object or image, it still influences behavior.

It's in the Bag

You are assigned to a new project and enter a room to meet the team.[40] Everyone sits and, as you begin discussing the task at hand, things feel notably abrasive. Why is everyone so confrontational and difficult? You can tell your new colleagues are holding back information and seem to be in it for themselves, which you fear will sabotage the project. Just to be safe, you keep your own good ideas hidden in your notebook in case there's an opportunity to share them when none of these conniving jerks could get credit for your hard work.

What if I told you there was something in that room that had made you all act more aggressive and confrontational toward your colleagues? Would you be surprised to learn that a simple briefcase (that you likely didn't even notice) influenced the behavior of everyone in the meeting? If only you had been assigned to the backpack group. None of them consciously noticed the bag either, but this particular study found they were much more cooperative than the teams in the briefcase room.

In another study,[41] students primed with the flash of a logo during a video (only thirty milliseconds, so the conscious brain couldn't realize it) were more creative in their tasks when shown the Apple logo than the IBM logo. Similarly, those who saw a Disney logo were much more honest in the subsequent tests than those who saw the logo for E!

A picture is worth a thousand words, but (as you learned in Part I of this book) a strong brand is powered by a million memories.

Smells

Adult humans can distinguish approximately ten thousand unique odors using forty million olfactory receptor neurons.[42] Like sight, our sense of smell evolved to help our species survive. Predators smell bad to us, and prey (also known as food) smells good. Naturally occurring things that can harm us are likely to have a smell we dislike, quickly alerting the brain to "get outta there!" as soon as possible. Because of a direct route to the limbic system, certain scents can trigger fight or flight while others bring up vivid memories, and another can make your mouth water.

While visuals occupy 70 percent of sensory perception, scent is tied much more directly to memory, which can make associations with it stronger.[43] People can remember a scent and its related memory with 65 percent accuracy after twelve months, while visual recall was only 50 percent accurate after just four months.

Scent has a direct path to emotions, which is directly tied to buying behavior. This is one reason so many big brands have scent logos.

If you aren't in marketing, you might not realize that the smells associated with your favorite brands aren't there by accident. Companies like ScentAir help businesses from restaurants to casinos identify their custom scents, which have been proven to increase retail sales by 11 percent, food quality satisfaction scores by 8 percent, and customer satisfaction scores by 20 percent.[44]

Scent is incredibly powerful. For example:

- Participants were three times as likely to clear away crumbs after an intentionally crumbly snack when there was a faint scent of cleaning products in the air[45]

- Diners are more likely to order seafood when there is a scent of lemon in the restaurant[46]

- People gambled 45 percent more in a casino with a pleasant smell[47]

- When reviewing shoes, 84 percent rated those in a floral-scented room as superior to (and valued them about ten dollars higher than) the exact same shoes in an unscented room[48]

- A convenience store that pushed the smell of coffee near the gas pumps enjoyed a 300 percent increase in coffee sales[49]

And our brains tend to associate our own emotions with the way a scent makes us feel. If you are needing to ask strangers for directions, stand in front of a bakery instead of a clothing store (they'll be much more willing to help you out).[50] Or perhaps invest in a body spray that smells like baking cookies or roasting coffee, as that can encourage the same generosity of spirit. In addition:

- Subjects performed information processing tasks faster and more accurately when their cubicles were diffused with rosemary essential oil[51]

- Volunteers solved puzzles 17 percent faster after exposure to floral fragrances[52]

- A quick whiff of vanilla before an MRI reduced anxiety for 63 percent of patients[53]

That Stinks

Nothing can kill an otherwise enjoyable experience faster than a foul odor in the air. Think about it: have you ever walked into a hotel room and had it smell like cigarette smoke? Or mold? Or mothballs? I think we all have (and, as a side note, did you feel your nose crinkle up a little at those words?).

Let's try again: "It was repulsive, the air was thick with the stink of moldy mildew and mothballs."

Anything? That shows the power of scent even when you can't smell!

There is no amount of luxurious furniture or great view in a hotel room that can overcome the smell of dead fish. Just like the smell of burned popcorn can keep an entire office from working for the day, the wrong smell can influence your customers to buy less and have a worse experience.

Sounds

Different emotional states can be triggered by sound to influence behavior.[54]

Let's say you own a restaurant—should you play fast, upbeat music or slow jams? It depends on your goals. If your goal is to increase table turnover (think smaller tickets), fast tunes will do the trick. If instead you are looking for higher prices paid per ticket, slower music will encourage them to linger and buy more (appetizer, drinks, dessert).[55] Understanding how you make money will make it easy to pull the right levers.

Slow music influences more than dining behavior. Grocery and retail stores also benefit from a more leisurely buying experience with fewer beats per minute. More time in the store means an increase in exposure to items and impulse buys.

Oh, and don't let employees pick the music. While they may not love the audio track of their workday, when music aligns with the brand, time in store increases by as much as twenty-two minutes (and purchase amounts are higher as well).[56]

What about familiar music? Customers reported that they shopped longer when they were exposed to familiar music—in reality, they were there longer when exposed to music they didn't know.[57]

What about the type of music? French music playing in the grocery store? You're more likely to try out a French wine (but don't worry, you'll be picking up a bottle of the German wine next week when the music changes).[58] And this goes beyond consumables. As Patrick Fagan, cofounder of Capuchin Behavioural Science, told me of a study he did in 2014, background noises influenced buying behavior on eBay as well.[59] Those listening to pop music and factual conversation (football commentary, economics reports) were more likely to make better purchases, while those listening to classical music overvalued the quality of items by 5 percent. Other distracting noises (restaurant chatter, babies crying) put people in a worse mood and negatively impacted their choices.

Touch

Merely touching an item greatly increases the ownership someone feels for it—and then the brain doesn't want to give it up,[60] triggering perceived ownership and loss aversion (Chapter 9).

And, because the subconscious is wired to seek out rewards, your brain constantly wants you to reach out and touch things.

Have you ever walked through a store and seen a cozy-looking sweater, soft blanket, or other item and felt compelled to touch it? You may not be in the market for a new throw, but this looks so soft and cozy. *Is it as soft as I think it is? Ooooh…that's so nice!* Before you know it, you have one for yourself and each of your friends or family members because you want to give that gift—that *feeling*—to others.

It's not a coincidence that you can see and touch the item in the box. Or that toys have a "press here" or "feel this" message on the outside with a big arrow. Blankets don't *need* to be packaged with an opening so you can feel the texture, but they often are. And while it is nice of them to let you "try before you buy," these companies know that touch increases purchases.

Similarly, getting people to try things on in a store greatly increases the likelihood they will buy them.

This may lead you to ask, "But how do I get them to physically touch the item in our online sales world?" With Amazon or other online advertising, does touch come into play before they can physically touch the item in question?

You bet it does. This is the power of touch without touch.

Let's do a little test. I want you to picture a leather couch. The description says, "material: leather" and leaves it at that.

Does it sound appealing? Do you want to touch or feel the couch? Are you interested in it at all? Probably not.

What about this: "Buttery soft and supple chocolate-brown leather"? Maybe that piques your interest a little more.

Well-chosen words can trigger your texture centers, so you are responding *as if you were touching it*—activating perceived ownership, loss aversion, and an increased likelihood of buying.[61]

The truth of the matter is this: touch—whether it is happening in your hands or simply in your mind—impacts sales. It is most impactful when someone can physically touch something, but if you can't get something in their hands, thoughtfully chosen words, sounds, and images make a big difference. (And don't forget about the power of mirror neurons! A video of someone experiencing the product can influence buying behavior too.)

Will You Hold This?

While walking across campus to be part of a study, participants unexpectedly bumped into someone with very full hands—books, a clipboard, papers—which fell to the ground. "Oops! So sorry. Can you hold this for a second while I pick these up?" A coffee cup, either hot or iced, was handed to the participant, who had no idea they were being primed. They went their merry way and checked in to the study. Their task was to read a story and give feedback and ratings on the person they read about.

And you won't believe what happened.

Those who held the cup of iced coffee rated a hypothetical person they read about as being colder, less social, and more selfish than the students who held the hot coffee.[62]

The totally unrelated scenario impacted their responses in the task. The main thing I want you to understand from this example is the very literal way the brain makes associations between concepts. Cold drink = cold hands = cold personality.

Whether you're using words, images, or smells, the brain makes these literal associations. Even something as simple as font size has been shown to benefit from this as well (small font = small price).[63]

It may seem logical to have the sale price in larger font, but when it's smaller, the amount feels smaller too.

Fonts can change the way you feel about a sentence. And that picture of a person drinking an iced coffee on the homepage of your website could be encouraging potential customers to give your offer the cold shoulder. I tell my clients all the time, whether you think about these things in advance or not, they can still be priming your potential customers. Wouldn't you rather have thought about the impacts of that word, image, or scent on the brain, and made sure it is properly aligned with your brand, before settling on one to use?

Words

One famous study had university students unscramble thirty sentences, which they were told was to test their language ability. One group was given neutral sentences. The other was primed with words that would be considered stereotypes of elderly people: Florida, old, gray, careful, sentimental, wise, bingo, forgetful, retired, wrinkle, ancient, helpless, and cautious.[64]

Upon completing the test, the facilitator told them how to get to the elevator to leave. Another person was sitting in the hall (it looked like they were waiting to speak to another professor, but they used a hidden stopwatch to time the participant from the time they left until they got to a specific spot on the floor).

And guess what they found?

Those primed with the elderly stereotype words took longer to get down the hallway!

This study also did a test with "rude" and "polite" priming words compared to a control group. Participants were each told to do their word scrambles, then come down the hall and find the professor when they were done to be given their next task. When they got there, the professor was having a conversation with another "student" (who was actually part of the experiment and had a stopwatch going), and they recorded how long people would wait before interrupting to get their next task. As you may have guessed, those in the rude group were more impatient than those in the control group (who were less patient than the polite group).

PARTICIPANTS WHO INTERRUPT

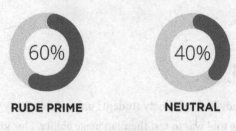

RUDE PRIME   **NEUTRAL**

POLITE PRIME

Those primed with rude words were much more likely to interrupt.

This next one tests two competing stereotypes that live within the same person. All participants were Asian-American female undergraduates at MIT, with similar SAT scores.[65] They were asked to fill out a pre-questionnaire with the priming words. One group was primed with female terms (Is your dorm co-ed or single-sex?), and the other group was primed with terms about being Asian-American (Do your parents or grandparents speak languages other than English?). Both were compared to a control group.

They were then given twenty minutes to complete a series of twelve difficult math problems.

Was there a difference in how many attempted questions these comparably capable young women answered correctly? You bet:

- Asian Identity: 54 percent

- Control: 49 percent

- Female Identity: 43 percent

I would guess that most (if not all) of these women would say they don't agree with the stereotypes in the test. They might consciously fight against them, but much like with the "toast" and "bread" phenomenon that kicked off the chapter, the subconscious brain's automatic association still impacts behavior. They were all equally capable, but being primed with a simple question meant an 11 percent reduction in scores.

How often are you inadvertently biasing surveys you send out to customers by asking priming questions too early? Are your company's new hire procedures setting some off on a worse path than others? Could one wrong statement at the beginning of a staff meeting be causing your team to perform 11 percent worse than they could if you chose your words more thoughtfully? These are the types of questions I help clients with, and what you can address and fix with the power of behavioral economics.

Memories

You already know scent is tied to memory, but other memory triggers can impact behavior in crazy (literal) ways. For example, participants asked to recall a time they betrayed a friend were twice as likely to take antiseptic wipes for their hands than those who were asked to remember times when they did a good deed.[66]

According to the researchers, this was the subconscious brain wanting to take any action to "cleanse" itself of these bad deeds. And the really crazy thing was, after wiping their hands, they were less likely to agree to volunteer their time because they had psychologically "wiped their hands clean" and were no longer burdened by the guilt.

The Power of the Prime

I can sum this chapter up in two words: *everything matters.*

This applies to the words and images on your own materials, as well as whatever was said or done right *before* the customer got to your brand assets.

While you can't control everything, it is worth looking at the things you can control.

What happened on the show right before your ad came up on a commercial break? Is your billboard placed in a stressful intersection, and how does that impact the association with your brand?

Because priming is so impactful, you will see it a lot in Part III: Pricing strategy. Website design. Advertisements. As you have seen in these priming examples, small things—just a few simple words, smells, or images—can make a huge difference.

And one of the most important things to remember is that, across all the studies, people said they were not influenced by the items. Or that they didn't see them at all. This is why understanding the concepts of behavioral economics is so critical: people cannot tell you what they will do and what influenced their choices.

When you create your materials and brand experience, consider all the senses, and combine as many as you can to align your primes. And remember that literal brain: Are big fonts making your prices seem bigger? What if you change a color here or an image there? It is important to try things in your own business to see what replicates with your audience. But before you jump into testing everything, keep moving through this book. There are many concepts to consider, and there is a right way to approach testing (as you'll see in Part III).

Applying Priming

Remember: Everything matters—choose images, words, smells, and other primes that align with your brand.

Try it Yourself: Consider your brand. If your customers could only know *one thing* about you, what would it be? Look for something that differentiates you from competitors (beyond "knowledgeable" or "friendly" staff). Do you empower people? Make them feel safe or secure? Help them achieve their dreams?

Use a thesaurus to help you find the perfect words to evoke that priming reaction: the ones you can *feel* when you read or hear them.

Next, find some images that reflect that one thing in various applications. What does empowerment look like when someone is using computer software? Or running their business?

Finding powerful priming images that support the one thing your brand is trying to embody can subtly move customers through the buying process and reinforce the impression that they have found the right fit for their needs.

More Priming

Find priming again in these chapters: The Truth About Pricing (22), How to Sell More of the Right Stuff (23), A Series of Small Steps (24), May I Take Your Order? (25), What Problem Are You Solving (26), The Power of Story (27)

Priming is one of my favorite concepts because it can be tested so easily. One new picture or updated word can change everything. Learn more about priming and other concepts from the chapter in these episodes of *The Brainy Business* podcast:

- **(Episode 18) Priming: Why You Should Never Have a Difficult Conversation with Someone Holding an Iced Coffee.** An expansion of what you've read in this chapter, with many more ways to apply priming in your business.

- **(Episodes 24–28) A series dedicated to each of the senses,** so you can learn even more about how sight, hearing, touch, taste, and smell really work, how they connect to the brain, and how your business can use them to build an amazing brand experience.

- **(Episode 89) Focusing Illusion: Why Thinking About Something Makes It Seem More Important Than It Is.** Want to know more about the numbers-on-the-clock phenomenon and how it is impacting your life and business every day? You'll love this episode.

CHAPTER 7

Anchoring and Adjustment

When your subconscious brain doesn't know the answer to something, it takes a guess. Some might call this an "educated" guess, but often it is working off rules of thumb—which is where all these concepts in behavioral economics come from. As it is processing at eleven million bits per second, it is using these judgment calls a lot to guide you through your day and life.

When introducing this concept, I always go with a little question-and-answer game. While I can't hear your responses, I am trusting you not to Google the answer. Just go with your gut. Ready?

Are there more or less than 10,000
emperor penguins in Antarctica?

How many do you think there are?

Do you have that number in your head?

There are 595,000 penguins in Antarctica! Was your number a lot *less* than that?

Let's try another one.

Are there more or less than 1,000 countries in the world?

How many do you think there are?

There are 195 countries in the world. Was your number *higher* than that?

What Happened?

Your subconscious took the number I threw out to you and assumed I must know something about emperor penguins or the number of countries in the world (which is why I **primed** you with that first number).

What if I had simply asked, "How many emperor penguins are there in Antarctica?" without the preface of "Is it more or less than 10,000?" Would your number have been different? Or what if the anchor I gave was 1 million? Or 10 million? 100 million?

When I asked the question about countries, your lazy brain's conversation with itself might have been something like, "Hmmm...let's see how many countries I can name. No...that's going to take too long, and it's a lot of work." If I hadn't given an anchor, it might have used some other rule of thumb—like estimating. You might have thought, "Well, I know North America has three, then there is Australia and New Zealand out there too... think of a map...maybe there is an average of 20 countries on each other continent? Or how about I pad that a little because I am probably forgetting a bunch...so let's say 30 per continent. That means 120 plus the handful I named, so I'll guess 125." Not too far off.

But because I gave you the high anchor of 1,000, your brain skipped that whole estimating thing and went with the easiest possible path:[67] "She must know something about countries, which is why she gave me that number to start with. That seems pretty high...but I don't know a lot of countries...I'll go with 600." (Or wherever you ended up.)

And this works with completely random numbers—ones that should have no impact on the question.

A few years ago, while giving a presentation to a group of female entrepreneurs, I asked everyone to think of the last two digits of their Social Security number. Then I asked them to look at my necklace—a particularly blingy piece—and to consider how much they thought I paid for it. And do you know what happened?

I explained to the audience, "Studies have shown[68] someone with a higher last two digits, like 8, 9, will value the item higher than someone with a lower last two digits, like 1, 2."

One woman raised her hand and said, "The last two digits of my Social Security number actually *are* 8, 9 (what are the odds!) and when you asked about the value I thought, eighty-nine dollars. And then I thought, no, that's stupid. I'll say sixty-five."

And that is exactly how anchoring and adjustment works.

(For the record, the woman with the lowest last two digits in the room valued the necklace much lower, at thirty-five dollars.)

The anchor (number placed into your brain up front) is a form of priming. With random things like the Social Security number, the effects can wear off quickly (so all the low-SSN folks aren't destined to be hagglers), and these types of numbers are really important to keep in mind for advertisements, presenting products on websites, setting prices for packages, and more.

The Snickers Example

It's funny how you get "known" for things when you talk about them on a podcast or in presentations. Ever since I started sharing this research study, it has resonated so much that people say, "It's like Melina's Snickers example!"[69] An article I wrote on this was the tenth most popular for that outlet for the entire year.[70] This is one of those magic examples people just *get*. So, here it is:

There were two nearly identical grocery store end-cap displays. The first said, "Snickers bars—buy *them* for your freezer" and the second said, "Snickers bars—buy *18* for your freezer." I think we can all agree that eighteen is a ridiculous number of Snickers bars to buy at once—not a common occurrence.

As someone in charge of the messaging, you would likely logic yourself out of putting this number on an ad. You might say, " *'Them'* is unlimited! Someone could get a hundred if they wanted." Or "People will ask how I came up with the number eighteen. I don't want to have to justify an arbitrary number. And it couldn't make that much of a difference anyway…"

The truth is it *does* make a difference. A huge one.

The sales of Snickers bars increased by 38 percent when the number eighteen was used instead of the word "them." 38 percent!

Why?

When you are walking through the store and you see an ad with the word "them" in it, it likely doesn't even register as a blip in your brain. If it does, you might think, "Sure, I'll get two or three" and drop them in the cart. But the number eighteen? That might stop your subconscious brain because it is such an unusual number. You might think, "Eighteen?! That's crazy. I'm way better than all those people who are buying eighteen candy bars. I'll just get six."

Did you see what happened there?

That is anchoring and adjustment at work. Consciously, we can be scared to throw out big numbers, but they can make a huge difference in sales because of the way they talk to the subconscious brain.

In addition, there's a very important shift in the **framing** of the question that hits the brain with this tiny change.

When you use the word "them," it becomes a fancy word for "zero," and the question being asked is "Do you want to buy Snickers?" Changing the word "them" to the number "18" assumes the sale. It subtly shifts the question you are asking to a much more valuable, "How many Snickers do you want to buy?" Adding the anchor by changing one word shifts the frame and the entire subconscious buying experience.

That same study from the *Journal of Marketing Research* details some other common anchoring techniques used in grocery stores.

Anchoring is why people buy more when items are marked as "10 for $10" than "$1 each."

It is also why placing a limit on something will make people buy more. This study had three conditions:

- 10 cents off soup!

- 10 cents off soup! (Limit 4)

- 10 cents off soup! (Limit 12)

What happened? Again, you might think those people who need to stock up on soup will stock up regardless, but that would be too logical!

When the number was unlimited, the average purchase was 3.3 cans of soup. With a limit of four? 3.5 cans—so it went up a little. What about with the limit of twelve? They doubled! An average of 7 cans purchased!

Crazy, but true.

Applying Anchoring and Adjustment

Remember: Don't be afraid of big numbers. Consider how a number may shift the **frame** of the question.

Try It Yourself: Find a vague piece of messaging and throw in a number to see how it impacts behavior. You can try big anchors (like eighteen Snickers) or small ones (to help a process feel easier or simpler, perhaps).

Start by defining the goal—what you want people to do after interacting with your piece of messaging.

Consider my choice of the number 1,000 when asking about countries. This was because I wanted you to come up with a higher number. If my goal was to get you close to 195, I might have chosen 250 or 200. Once you know your goal, you can determine which type of anchor you want (low or high) and test some out!

More Anchoring

Find anchoring again in these chapters: The Truth About Pricing (22), How to Sell More of the Right Stuff (23), A Series of Small Steps (24), May I Take Your Order? (25)

Anchoring is such a fun concept to play with, because (as you learned in the chapter about framing) there is so much power in a well-placed number. It is so easy to start testing with, and you can start immediately. (But before you do, read the next chapter on relativity, as these two concepts are like milk and cookies: they are often found together.) Listen to this episode of *The Brainy Business* podcast to deepen your knowledge of anchoring:

- **(Episode 11) Anchoring and Adjustment: The One Word That Increased Sales 38 Percent.** There is so much more to anchoring than candy bars and countries. This episode is chock-full of my suggestions for ways to use the concept in a jewelry store, in real estate, furniture sales, car sales, or service-based businesses, inside a company, for nonprofits, and more!

CHAPTER 8

Relativity

Humans can't value one-off items—we need a comparison point to know if it is a good or a bad deal. And I don't think anyone has put this concept better than my friend Brian Ahearn, whose book *Influence PEOPLE* helps you remember this concept with the phrase[71] "There is nothing high or low but comparing makes it so."

And, to paraphrase the fantastic example from that book, let's say you go into a furniture store and see a couch you're interested in. You ask the sales rep, "Excuse me, how much is that couch?" and they respond, "Nine hundred dollars. Oh, oops! My mistake, *seven* hundred dollars."

In that example, seven hundred dollars feels like a great deal, but what if, instead, when you asked, "How much is that couch?" their response was, "Five hundred dollars. Oh, oops! My mistake, *seven* hundred dollars." Feels a lot worse now, right?

The price of the couch never changed. It was never either of the other two prices, but the way you *feel* about it is completely different. And the only thing that changed was the context; the item just before set an **anchor** that made the couch feel like something you were excited about buying or like a waste of money.

The Value of Fifteen Dollars

Is the value of fifteen dollars always the same? Or does it shift from one context to the next?

Scenario One: You are at a store and pick out a spatula you want to buy. It is sixteen dollars. While in line, you remember seeing the exact same spatula at a store across town for a dollar. Do you put it back and go to the other store to buy the cheaper spatula? Or do you proceed with your purchase?

Scenario Two: You are redoing the living room and find the perfect rug. It is $500. While you're standing in line, someone says, "You know, you can get that exact same rug for only $485 at the shop across town." Do you put it back and drive across town to buy the less expensive rug? Or do you go ahead and buy it now?

If you are like most people, you would have said you wanted to put back the spatula and drive across town to save fifteen dollars…but you would not do the same thing with the rug. Why?

In "logical" conventional economics, a dollar (or in this case, fifteen dollars) should elicit the exact same behavior for you regardless of the item it is attached to. But, of course, it doesn't.

The relative price of the item impacts your behavior—fifteen dollars compared to one dollar feels like much more than fifteen dollars compared to five hundred dollars—but why does that matter? The truth is…it shouldn't. If our brains were more logical, the real question would be, "What does fifteen dollars mean to me compared to the time to drive across town?"[72]

Years ago, while running the marketing department at a financial institution, I wrote a blog post about gas prices and auto loan payments. It is common for people to drive out of their way for "cheaper" gas; I know some people who will drive an extra ten minutes to save ten cents per gallon. Let's say you have a car with a fifteen-gallon tank. You are saving $1.50 if your gas tank is completely empty when you get there to fill up. And, of course, I will not try to estimate just how much gas you are burning up to save that $1.50, but I am willing to guess it is enough to eat into at least some of that "gain."

We regularly ran a promotion where we would refinance an existing auto loan and beat the rate by 1 percent (which is what prompted me to write the post I am referencing). Many people—the same ones who would drive out of their way to save ten cents a gallon—would say, "1 percent isn't worth the time to fill out the application and refinance. How much could it really save?" (We humans are notoriously bad at comparing things across categories like this.)

Using a simple online calculator, if you had a $20,000 auto loan at 8 percent interest, you would pay $10 more a month than if it was at 7 percent interest. So, you could save $120 a year by taking a few minutes to fill out the application online and refinance the car—probably in less time than it would take to drive to the "cheap" gas station and fill up the tank.

Finding a way to communicate that in our advertising was key in getting people to apply and save (a win-win). While many of the behavioral nudges presented in this book are showing you ways to work with the subconscious (and not alert the conscious brain), this is an example where you want to shock the brain enough to make your message become salient (stand out enough to be noticed). Helping someone discover that their behavior (driving ten minutes to save ten cents per gallon) is inefficient and ineffective compared to the one-and-done quick application that will save hundreds requires them to be ready to process the relative values. A surprising picture or curiosity-inducing subject line on an email can **prime** them to be ready to receive the information and invest the few minutes to apply now.

Retail Examples

If you own a shop of some kind, you should absolutely incorporate relativity into your layout and pricing plan.

Let's say you decided to do your back-to-school shopping at Target, because they have a little bit of everything—school supplies and clothes at affordable prices. On your way in, you see a kid's T-shirt near the door for ninety-nine dollars. You might think, "Whoa, Target's prices have gone way up. I'm not sure if I can afford to buy here this year," and when you get to the clothes section, you are pleased to see the shirts are on sale and around forty dollars each, so you stock up and get three because that was just a little more than the price of one shirt regularly!

But was it?

What if I told you the shirts were twenty-five dollars each last year? Relative to twenty-five dollars, forty dollars seems high. However, the store placed something even more expensive—the ninety-nine dollar shirt—to reset your **anchor** and establish a new relative price, so now forty dollars seems like a great deal. They don't want you to buy the ninety-nine-dollar shirt (I mean, they would be happy if you *did*, but that isn't its purpose). Its sole purpose in life is to make the other price seem low—so you feel better about buying.

> **Is it ethical?**
>
> There are many papers addressing the ethics of the field, and it is not addressed again in this book. My general approach is that any knowledge can be used for "evil" in the hands of the wrong person. It is my hope and intent that everyone will use the powers given to them here for good. Err on the side of helping people improve their lives, and please nudge responsibly.

Espresso?

Imagine you own an electronics store and decide to carry an espresso machine. You do not have any other coffee-related items, so you place it between a microwave and a blender. It is tagged at $150. You were confident people would snatch it up, but it just sits there. And sits there. After six months, you haven't sold a single one.

What do you do?

Before picking up this book, you probably would have figured you had two options: 1) pull it from the shelves and give up on espresso machines or 2) discount the heck out of it.

Both of those approaches are wrong.

What you should do is get another espresso machine that looks very similar to the one you already have, but twice the size and twice the price, and set it right next to the $150 one. Now, when people come by, they will see two espresso machines and have something to compare. They might think, "Well, $300 is a lot to invest in an espresso machine, but this *other* one is so nice and compact, it could fit on my counter, and look at the color! That's only a few trips to Starbucks to make up the difference in price. Eventually I could upgrade to the bigger model if I want, but this is a nice introductory item…and it's such a great deal…"

Boom. Espresso machine sold.[73]

The Calorie Conundrum

When you finish an hour-long spin class or run a 5K, you feel like you have done a ton of work. You are sweating and feel like you really *earned* it, right? A lot of people will then celebrate by eating a little extra or saying, "It's okay to have that snack because I ran today." Our brains relate the effort expended to run with the effort expended to snack and, for many, that valuation is way off.

Once, many years ago, logging my workout into a fitness tracker, I was on top of the world. It felt like I totally killed it: it said I burned three hundred calories and I thought, "Yes! I'm awesome!"

Until I noticed the little conversion chart, which let me know that my sweat-fest was equal to 1.25 bottles of soda or a single slice of pizza. Let me tell you, it did *not* make me want to celebrate with a food-related treat! And it made the comparison much more real. One study by Johns Hopkins put this to good use.[74] They posted signs in convenience stores which read, "You have to run fifty minutes to burn off the calories in one bottle of soda." (Yikes!)

They were pleased to see the consumption of sugary drinks among teenagers fall when the signs were out. So, just know that relativity isn't all about pricing. Finding the right point of relativity (adding **context**) can encourage healthier behavior, which is awesome.

But be careful with the comparisons you choose to make. Something that seems like an obviously great relative message for you won't necessarily motivate your target market to change their behavior. As an example, consider an ad, which was meant to encourage people to drink less soda and went viral in 2019 for the wrong reason.[75] It asked, "would you eat six donuts?" thinking that would shock the viewer, but the internet was quickly filled with excited tweets about how many donuts people felt they could consume guilt-free.

It is important to understand your audience and speak their language when looking to nudge behavior (more on this in Chapter 13). When you don't take the time to test concepts (Chapter 28), it can result in epic fails like this one, which backfired and, instead of getting people to stop drinking soda, made them feel like it was healthy to gorge on donuts.

Applying Relativity

Remember: Context determines value—it's all relative.

Try It Yourself: Product offerings are the easiest way to apply relativity. We will talk about this much more in Part III, but to test for now, consider your best product or service offering.

- What is included in it?

- What are the benefits and what problem does it solve?

- Do you have a "$300 espresso machine" comparison point (i.e., something similar, but clearly a worse value, that people can evaluate to help them see the value of the best offer)? If not, create it now (and set it up with a high anchor) to help make the best offer look good.

Don't worry about being perfect right now; just write out your thoughts and keep them handy.

More Relativity

Find relativity in these chapters: The Truth About Pricing (22), How to Sell More of the Right Stuff (23), A Series of Small Steps (24), May I Take Your Order? (25)

Businesses need to understand and properly apply relativity to show their value. Learn more about it in these episodes of *The Brainy Business* podcast:

- **(Episode 12) Relativity: The Brain Can't Value One-Off Items.** Includes a walk-through of setting up your product offerings so they are using relativity and anchoring in the best way possible.

- **(Episode 8) What Is Value?** What can your business learn from a $214 grilled cheese? A lot.

CHAPTER 9

Loss Aversion

It will probably not surprise you to learn that people hate to lose things. If you have ever had or seen small children playing, you have experienced this firsthand.

Take the two littles in our house. Older brother is playing contentedly in the playroom, surrounded by far too many toys for anyone to enjoy at once. Little sister wanders up to a toy on the periphery, far outside the immediate reach of older brother. "Noooo!" he screams as the tears well up, "I was just about to play with that!" Somehow, this random toy—which could be anything from an empty box to a Transformer to a Barbie—has now become his absolute favorite and he cannot give it up. Though none of the other toys are great candidates to hand over to little sister, either. He does not want to lose the opportunity to play with *any* of them.

We parents know and talk about how ridiculous it is. And yet, your subconscious brain does this exact same thing all day, every day. We never really unlearn this behavior; we simply figure out how to control it outwardly.

Your subconscious brain is basically a two-year-old throwing a tantrum and freaking out when someone else tries to play with your Wonder Woman doll—even if you weren't using it at that exact moment.

Sad, but true.

Losses or Gains?

So, what have we done in our businesses and society? Gotten it completely backward, unfortunately. We have looked at this behavior and said, "People like things, so we should give them more things!"

We have created a gain-riddled society built on punch cards and reward programs intended to create loyalty, but that typically sit gathering dust between the driver's seat and the center console in the car.

Gains are not the key to driving behavior—losses are. (And before you object with, "But I don't want to be negative or fear-based," don't worry, as you'll see, it doesn't have to be.)

To show you how it feels, I want you to imagine two different scenarios. Really try to put yourself in the moment of each. They are simple, I promise.

Scenario One: One morning, you grab a jacket you haven't worn in a while. While putting it on, you realize there's twenty dollars in the pocket. Amazing!

How do you feel? Probably pretty good; this doesn't happen every day. You might tell a couple of people about it, or maybe not. Will you still be bragging about it tomorrow? Or next week? Will you remember, the next time you grab this jacket, that it was the one with twenty dollars in the pocket? Or next year, when you have the same chilly-weather experience? Probably not.

Scenario Two: Imagine you're going to an event that only takes cash. You do some quick mental math and decide a hundred dollars is more than enough for the full day—you will probably have some money left over. You swing by the ATM on your way, and when you stop to pay for parking, you realize there are only four bills there! You look in the abyss between the seats, check your wallet again—are two stuck together, maybe? No. You have *lost* twenty dollars. How does that feel?

Pretty terrible, I'm guessing. Will you tell people about *this* experience? Will you remember it every time you use that parking lot? Or see advertisements for that event? Or use that ATM? Might you even blame the bank or credit union for "stealing" twenty dollars from you when it wasn't their fault? Will this become a story you tell your grandkids about someday?

Maybe it will not be that extreme, but I'm confident you felt it more than the joy of the "found" twenty dollars. And why? Shouldn't it feel the same, since it is the same amount of money? That is what conventional economics would say, but if traditional economic models were always accurate, behavioral economics would not exist!

The Economics of Loss

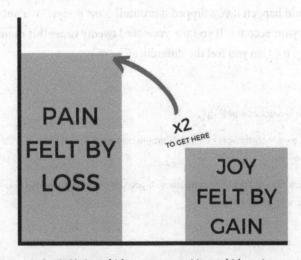

It takes double the joy felt from a gain to equal the pain felt from a loss.

The forefathers of the field, Daniel Kahneman and Amos Tversky (among others), have found there is a science to this.

The research shows it takes double the joy felt from a gain to equal the pain felt from a loss,[76] which has been seen across all sorts of industries and applications. Here are a couple of examples to show how it can work without feeling negative.

Credit Cards

Lots of financial institutions send out promotional messages like, "Swipe your card twenty times this month and we will give you fifty dollars." That is a very generous offer, but many people do not take advantage of things like this. You might have gotten these in the mail and thought, "Oooh, fifty dollars, I'm definitely going to do that!" Then, three months later, you stumble across the flyer and think, "Darn, I must have forgotten. Next time I'll *definitely* take advantage of it." And just like that, it's back out of your brain's processing.

What would happen if you flipped it around? Now it says, "We put fifty dollars in your account. If you use your card twenty times this month, you get to keep it." Can you feel the difference?[77]

> Which is more compelling?
>
> "Swipe your card twenty times this month and we will give you fifty dollars."
>
> "We put fifty dollars in your account. If you use your card twenty times this month, you get to keep it."

Switching the message from a gain to a loss is a form of **framing**, which you learned about in Chapter 5.

Incentives

So many incentives are given after completing a task, but is that the best way? Binit Kumar, head of customer marketing at Zydus Wellness, shared an example with me of incentivizing sales staff in rural India.[78] In the traditional model, staff hit their targets 40–45 percent of the time. Then they did things a little differently. Each salesperson was handed a big check for the full incentive and told the money was already in their account—if they missed the target, the prepaid amount would be deducted from a future check.

This time, 70 percent hit their sales targets.

Motivation

Have you ever put too many items on your to-do list and had to roll some over to the next day? Perhaps the better question is, have you ever *not* had this happen (and actually completed everything you planned)? Due to optimism bias, which you will learn more about in Part IV, people tend to overcommit themselves and never quite learn the lesson. This creates a perpetual I-didn't-hit-the-goal-this-week-but-promise-to-do-better-next-time problem. Whether you are motivating yourself or looking to incentivize others on your team (or perhaps clients, if you are a coach or personal trainer), you can use loss aversion to your advantage with my jar method.

Instead of trying to talk to the conscious brain, the jar method adjusts the approach and appeals to the subconscious elephant.

Here's how my jar method works (outlined for a coach working with clients): First, get a bunch of clear glass jars—I like the ones with the chalkboard labeling spot—and write the name of one client on each jar. Next time you meet with them, say, "See this jar with your name on it? Every week you complete what you say you will, I'll put $10 in the jar. If you ever miss, I'll empty the entire jar and you start over. Whatever is in there at the end of the year, you get to keep." (In case your lazy brain didn't want to do that math, that would be $520 by the end of the year if they hit their goals each week.)

Every time you meet with them (whether in person or by videoconference), you want that jar to be in sight. You don't necessarily need to call attention to it, but the visual with their name and the money inside will be continually **priming** them and reminding them of the goal and commitment they've made. As a result, people are more likely to set realistic goals they will actually achieve, which creates a virtuous cycle (and helps you be more successful as their coach). It's a simple change and a win-win. (And, good news, there are several tips for you to overcome your own tendency to overcommit in Part IV.)

Cars

Think about the last time you went shopping for a car. Did they say this? "Here is the baseline model, which we used to calculate your monthly payment. Now, here are all the features you can add: power windows, leather seats, sunroof, navigation. Choose all of what you want to add, and we will increase your payment as we go!"

Or did they say something like this? "Here is the model we recommend for you, and here's the monthly payment," and if you balked at the price, "Here is the list of all the features—let me know which you want to remove."

They, of course, do the latter, because people buy cars with more features when the loss aversion is properly placed.[79] In the first version, the loss aversion is about the money in your bank account ("I can do without a backup camera to save $200").

In the second scenario, the loss is about the really cool car your subconscious brain has already decided you own. "Well, a backup camera would be nice, and $200 over sixty months is only $3.33—I'll use it enough to get $5 of value every month!"

Associating the proper ownership in the value proposition is critical to having loss aversion work to your advantage when presenting offers, whether it's a new car or a candy bar.

Increasing Healthy Behaviors

Let's say you have a goal to walk more (as most of us do). So you buy a fitness tracker and plan to hit your 10,000 steps each day. How long until you burn out on that dream and are no longer motivated? What if your phone had a setting such that, if you *didn't* hit your step goal that day, you would be blocked from all your nonessential apps (social media, maps, games) for the rest of the day? Or, what if your phone would automatically send a text message to your mom if you didn't complete your steps (or, say, take your medications) on time?

Might you be more inclined to stick to your plans in those scenarios?

You aren't alone, Aline Holzwarth explained to me.

Aline, the head of behavioral science at Pattern Health and principal at Dan Ariely's Center for Advanced Hindsight at Duke University, led a series of experiments to understand how loss aversion could fuel adherence among people looking to exercise more, eat well, and take their medication. She found that when participants could lose access to their smartphone apps as a result of non-adherence, they were more likely to stick to their health plans.[80] The threat of losing access to Twitter was enough to motivate them to get off the couch and get in those extra steps!

We can also be motivated to change our behavior to keep others (even digital others) from being punished. Do you remember Tamagotchi?[81] These were all the rage for a few months when I was in school; my friends and I each had at least one pixelated pet on a keychain that you had to feed and take care of all day long. If you neglected it for too long (say, while in class), it would get angry or get sick and die. Preventing the death of that Tamagotchi was paramount, and in an age before cell phones were common, many of us would risk a quick reach into the backpack to care for the pet and ensure it survived until the bell rang.

Knowing this fascinating phenomenon, Pattern Health has created a virtual pet that responds to users' behavior—when you complete your daily health tasks, the pet does fine. But if you fall off track, the pet suffers too.[82]

Virgil the Turtle needs your help!

Just as with the Tamagotchi of my youth, people are motivated to take care of others—even a virtual pet like Virgil the Turtle. (Virgil is the name that Pattern Health gave their mascot, but users name their own pets in order to strengthen their bond.) And users do get quite attached to their virtual pets. The drive to keep their pets happy helps Pattern Health's users stick to their goals. When Virgil can tell you are about to miss a commitment, he gets scared and hides in his shell. When you complete a task, he celebrates with you! The fear of losing Virgil (or having him upset with you) is enough to encourage people to take their medications or complete other health tasks.

Don't Get Too Extreme

You have probably noticed many companies have started using loss aversion to persuade people to sign up for lists by upping the ante. Instead of simply saying, do you want to subscribe, yes or no, they say things like, "Do you want to subscribe?"

- "Yes"

- "No, I don't care about saving money."

The good ones are subtle, but these can go bad quick.

The most ridiculous one I've seen was for a fitness DVD where you would only pay shipping and handling; it was trying to upsell other programs before the initial transaction was complete. The options were either:

- "Yes! Add The Total Body Fat Burning DVD Series To My Order For The One-Time Investment Of Only $25"

- "No thanks. I'm not interested in quickly obtaining my dream body. I understand this is my only opportunity to get access to this information and I'm ok with missing out. I understand that after declining this offer it may never be available again at any price...even if I wish to pay more I will pass on this forever."

Ha! Is that extreme or what? And long. Reading this makes most brains say, "I bet they would let me buy it if I really wanted it," or "I'll show you!" Loss aversion presents a fine line between working with the brain's subconscious rules and setting off all the alarm bells. Go too extreme, and you are likely to get rejected (and possibly damage your brand).

As a rule, my advice is to not try to trick people with any of the interventions you learn about in this book (it's all about helpful, ethical applications). Instead, aim to create awesome products and services they would love to have and use behavioral economics concepts to help them see why it will benefit them. It always works out better this way.

Applying Loss Aversion

Remember: It takes twice the joy felt from a gain to equal the pain felt from a loss.

Try It Yourself: Using nonnegative loss aversion is a type of framing. Take these common gain-focused messages and rewrite them in a way that incorporates loss aversion.

I'll kick it off with a reminder of an example from earlier in the chapter. Instead of saying, "Use your card twenty times this month and we'll give you fifty dollars," you can reframe it to say, "We put fifty dollars in your account; use your card twenty times and you can keep it." Now you try:

Buy Ten Get One Free _____

Hit your sales goals and you'll get a $500 bonus _____

Add one of your own _____

More Loss Aversion

Find loss aversion in these chapters: The Truth About Pricing (22), The Power of Story (27)

Reframing messages to incorporate loss aversion takes a little practice, and your conscious brain might rebel against it at first because there are so many examples of gains out there! It will feel like the gain messaging is best, but trust me: incorporating losses can be even more powerful. If you could double the benefits just by stating the message a little differently, why wouldn't you? Loss aversion has a dedicated episode of *The Brainy*

Business podcast to deepen your knowledge and get more tips for applying it in business:

- **(Episode 9) Loss Aversion: Why Getting New Stuff is Not the Same.** The original behavioral economics foundations episode. It includes additional application opportunities and more detail on the studies the concept is based upon.

CHAPTER 10

Scarcity

Pappy Van Winkle bourbon is one of the most difficult bottles in the world to find. While Jim Beam makes 84 million bottles a year, Pappy will allegedly only produce 84,000. If you can find a coveted twenty-three-year bottle retail (don't bother, you can't), it'll cost $270. If you ever do encounter one—and can convince its owner to part with it—expect it to run you about $3,000.[83]

In conventional economics, scarcity occurs when an item has limited availability (low supply), but unlimited desire (high demand) for that item. This can include natural resources, like oil and water, or more abstract things, like time. Time is a very scarce resource we all wish we had more of. And, while scarcity exists in every resource in some way or another (nothing is truly unlimited), what happens when we know something is scarce?

That is where *behavioral* economics steps in (and unconsumed bottles of Pappy sit on shelves collecting dust).

One study showed an advertisement for the same watch with two different descriptions: one said "New edition. Many items in stock." And the other version said, "Exclusive limited edition. Hurry, limited stock."[84]

What do you think happened?

People were willing to pay 50 percent more when ads said the watch was scarce—an exclusive limited edition with limited stock—than when there were "many in stock."

Remember, the watch is *exactly the same* in both cases.

Think about stamps. Even with regular price increases, they are still worth about fifty cents apiece, unless they are printed with errors. Did you know the most valuable stamp in the world, the British Guiana, is valued at $11.5 million? Why so expensive? It was a limited run and is the only one known to be in existence—but (sorry if you collect stamps), who cares?

What about the first silver dollar issued by the US government? It's called the "Flowing Hair" silver and copper dollar, and it sold for $10 million at auction. It was printed over two years (1794 or 1795) and was the first issued after the federal mint was established. What about the ones issued the next year? The 1796 Draped Bust Dollar is valued at just $794 (which is still a lot considering it is a *one-dollar coin*), unless it is in "certified mint state," where it could be worth as much as $59,548.

Scarcity and value are closely tied together—and for some reason, our crazy brains think less equals more in this case.[85] And, yes, scarcity is closely tied to, but not the same as, loss aversion.

Stock Up Before It's Gone

If you're a Costco member, you likely buy all sorts of things from them. They promote stocking up on your favorite items, not just because they are available in bulk, but because they might not be there if you come back tomorrow. This is a scarcity mindset.

If you own a retail store, it might be hard to think about copying this. Can you imagine? A customer comes in and asks for something they saw and wanted yesterday (or an hour ago), and you say, "Sorry, we're all sold out. Things go really fast around here." And then you don't move heaven and earth to find the item for them because it is gone and you know that, eventually, they will learn, just like everyone else.

Of course, customer service still matters; you should be helpful and friendly, but scarcity can only take effect when items are truly limited (meaning not everyone gets one).

Costco's approach works well because it is complemented by a fantastic return policy. This removes the fear of regret and makes it easy to buy a few extra items, because those purchased items can always be returned if they don't work out, and people know they are better safe than sorry. If you can ever provide a satisfaction guarantee, it is a great thing to have and promote. Most people do not end up using them, so the benefit is worth the risk.

> 100 percent satisfaction guarantees are always a good idea. They help people to overcome the fear of regret and give you a try now. Studies have shown that businesses are almost always better off with one prominently displayed than without.[86] Fewer people than you think will take advantage of a return policy like this, and the additional sales you get (especially when paired with a scarcity message) will far outweigh the returns.

The Official Drink of Fall

Starbucks has made three little letters synonymous with fall: PSL (or the full name, Pumpkin Spice Latte). Despite its popularity, the drink is only available for a few weeks each year.

Scarce items take on a life of their own. Did you know @therealPSL had 110,000 followers on Twitter? The account's post from August 28, 2018, saying, "Signing on just to say I'm back. Let's catch up IRL" got 2,300 likes, 654 retweets and 88 replies.[87]

Scarcity can create cult followings—which means other people do the marketing for you. They get excited and talk and spread the word on your behalf, making the brand bigger than anything you could do on your own. Word of mouth is a powerful thing, and scarcity can be a big driver of it.

Consider another Starbucks invention that took the world by storm: the Unicorn Frappuccino.

Unlike many scarce items at Starbucks, which are available for a month or so, the Unicorn Frappuccino was only going to be in stores for five days; in many locations, it sold out in less than two with almost no marketing (a couple of tweets and a single press release the day it came out). Apparently, the Unicorn Frappuccino announcement was leaked a week or so in advance and basically broke the internet.

Starbucks has a legacy of scarce items driving traffic into its stores—including its red cups, which get people around the globe jumping to be the first to post a coveted red cup selfie online each year. When you combine scarcity with social media, it can have amazing results—more on this in the next two chapters on herding and social proof.

Scarcity-Inducing Words

There are some words that automatically trigger scarcity in the brain of the consumer, like:

- Limited time
- Extended
- Custom
- Hand-crafted
- One of a kind
- Closeout sale

- Everything must go
- Last chance

If you do a promotion or discount, make sure it is short-term and remind people when it ends.

These terms can be added to both products and services. The brain sees these scarcity terms and thinks:

- "There is only one of these in the world? I better act quick so no one else snaps it up!"

- "Only two seats left at this price, and eight other people are searching for flights to Chicago right now? I must buy first!!"

- "Only one spot left on the calendar this month? I better grab it because she is probably the best around if she is in such high demand."

Remember, time is a valuable commodity, and you have a limited amount to give.

Instead of saying you are "very busy but will work to squeeze someone in," there is often value in holding firm on hours (just as Costco does on availability). Think of a doctor's office, massage therapist, or dentist—when their time is booked, it's booked. Sometimes that means scheduling a few months out. This makes you feel your doctor's time is more valuable, and you are also less likely to cancel appointments, which is a bonus for the clinic as well.

If you say, "I only have one spot available on my calendar next week, would you like to book that now?" the mind starts to get a little scared and doesn't want to lose the opportunity.

Applying Scarcity

Remember: Less available equals more value.

Try It Yourself: The easiest place for anyone to apply scarcity, regardless of industry or job role, is with their own time. We humans tend to overcommit and feel like we have to bend over backward to accommodate requests. Make a decision about your calendar—perhaps no meetings after five o'clock or no-meeting Thursdays—and stick to it. When people ask if you are available on Thursday, it is okay to respond with, "Thursday doesn't work, but how about eleven o'clock Friday?"

Fight the urge to overexplain or justify *why* you are busy, while still being kind and helpful in the response.

Saying, "Well, I can't Thursday because I have this all-day client meeting and Wednesday is no good either because…" is a long way of telling someone they aren't as important to you as those other things you are doing. When you don't provide the story of the other stuff going on, it is a non-issue and helps the scarcity speak for itself, which adds value. It is okay to be busy and unavailable at the first time someone proposes. You do not need to apologize for it. Scarcity in your time will help people value it (and you) more, especially if you are generous in your response.

More Scarcity

Find scarcity in this chapter: The Truth About Pricing (22)

Scarcity is one of those concepts everyone *knows*, but very few properly take advantage of. We all have so many scarce resources, and when they are **framed** well, it can encourage behavior while helping people feel more valued. Scarcity is showcased in these episodes of *The Brainy Business* podcast:

- **(Episode 14) Scarcity: Why We Think Less Available Means More Value.** Starbucks, Disney, Costco, and the amazing story of diamonds (did you know they aren't really scarce?) are all featured in this fun episode.

- **(Episode 47) Costco: A Behavioral Economics Analysis.** Learn from the best and see how Costco uses scarcity combined with other important behavioral economics concepts to provide value. Plus tips for using the lessons from their model in your business (and how to know if it is not a fit for you).

- **(Episode 73) Starbucks: A Behavioral Economics Analysis.** This follows a similar approach to the Costco episode, and quickly soared through the rankings to become the third most downloaded episode of *The Brainy Business*.

CHAPTER 11

Herding

If you place two identical food sources an equal distance from a colony of ants,[88] they will tend to choose one over the other—members of the group will follow each other back to the same source again and again while the second remains untouched.

Logically, this makes no sense—why ignore the wide-open food source? But humans do the same thing. Our herding brains choose restaurants by online reviews and crowdedness. Say you're in a new city and can only use street view to choose your fate. Most people would choose a full restaurant over an empty one. The reason? Your brain says, "They must know something I don't. The empty restaurant must be bad and the full one must be worth the forty-five-minute wait."

This is herd mentality at work.

Humans herd in the same way as other species—including cattle, wasps, and schools of guppies—for the same selfish reasons.[89]

Animals herd for protection. Anyone on the periphery is more likely to be killed by a predator than those on the inside, so it is beneficial to be as close to the center of the herd as you can. If you watch videos of sheep being herded by dogs, the animals on the outside run very fast to try and get to the middle, while those in the center are less inclined to move—until they find they've drifted too far out.

They also follow each other almost blindly, the assumption being, *If everyone is running in this direction, they must know something I don't. Instead of waiting around to see what they are running from, I will run first and ask questions later.*

Humans do this too. It is in our nature. I noticed this while trying to adapt to the flow of traffic while on a business trip in London. Most locals walk across the street whenever they can. Once someone started to move, others waiting on the sidewalk began to look noticeably uncomfortable. Some started to go without looking—only to be pulled back by someone else to keep them from being hit by an oncoming car. As more people crossed the street before the light changed, you could see those still on the corner getting more and more anxious, debating whether they should go too. This happens all over—look for it next time you are waiting in a crowd to cross the street.

This is also why nearly every teenager in the world has said something like, "But *Mom!* All my friends are doing it." To which Mom replied, "If all your friends were going to jump off a bridge, would you do that too?" That feeling of discomfort from not doing what everyone else is doing—whether it is going to a concert or staying in a hotel after prom, or being the last one to cross the street—is fueled by herding instinct.

We also learn by herding, thanks to those mirror neurons you read about in Part I. Learning by observation is critical to the survival and growth of our species. Babies watch adults and other children do things and emulate them almost immediately. This is how we learn to speak and walk and be safe and find food. It is critical to our survival.

This is also why restaurants and coffee shops seed their tip jars to make it look like others have already left tips. People are more likely to leave a tip when others have done the same. As you see from the image, I've also seen this tactic at many museums collecting donations in giant, clear containers throughout the space. (Remember the loss aversion jar? Clear containers work!)

Giant clear-sided boxes at the museum in London to encourage donations.

Have you ever been checking out at the grocery store and had the screen bring up a prompt asking if you want to donate to a cause? Clicking "no" makes you feel a twinge of guilt. Maybe you look around to make sure no one sees you press the big red *X*.

Taking it a step further, sometimes the person working the register will ask you if you want to donate to the cause, and your "No" must be uttered aloud. (The horror!)

You could just leave it at that, but people are often inclined to give an explanation. In a line recently, the woman ahead of me was asked by the lady working the register if she wanted to donate a dollar to the troops.

Her answer? "No, I do a lot of volunteer work at home and send lots of donations to the troops on my own, so I don't need to do that now."

Does the lady working the register care? It isn't her cause, after all. I'm sure it is corporate policy to ask everyone. She probably doesn't even like asking that question. Or maybe the woman giving the response thought those of us in line were judging her. She was inclined to think the rest of the herd would donate, and she needed a reason to explain why she was choosing not to. It made her feel better even though it did not matter to anyone else there.

Herding mentality is much more likely to come out when people feel vulnerable or are unsure of themselves. I know nothing about that woman in line, but it is very possible she does not *actually* volunteer or do anything for the troops. If that is the case, why would she say that? To overcome her natural tendency to feel she needs to go with the group; to avoid that guilt. When asked if they want to donate, many people get antsy, just like those on the sidewalk who don't want to be the last to cross. It's their herding brain taking over.

There are, of course, many other times when we are motivated by herding; we are more likely to rely on it when we are unsure of the best choice and lack confidence or feel there is a big risk if we mess up. This is why investing is full of examples of herding instincts gone wrong.[90]

Let's say your peers are all betting on a "sure thing." Would you be able to stand up to the group and bet on the opposite? Many people have a hard time with this because our brains prefer to be conventionally wrong than unconventionally right. In other words, if you bet and come up wrong, but everyone else did too, you are much less likely to be ridiculed than if you went against everyone else and made a losing bet that no one else made.

Imagine you are brought into a meeting of your peers with a large corporation that wants to invest in some smart people like you, and they are using this group interview to find the best of the best. You sit down and are shown a slide with a very simple equation on it, say "What does two plus two equal?" You are the eighth person in the group and, as each person ahead of you answers four, four, four, you follow suit. Easy.

There are a couple more rounds of this and then, another seemingly simple question, "What color do you get if you mix red and yellow?" You had an immediate answer in your head and were confident until the first person said "purple" with absolute confidence. "Purple?" You think. "How ridiculous." Then the next person says purple. And the next. And the next. You are getting anxious now. You thought it was orange, but these people must know something you don't. It's almost your turn—what will you say? Purple or orange?

Studies show that up to 75 percent of participants will give an answer they *know is wrong* to go with the group.[91] You might say you wouldn't do it, but in the heat of the moment, your subconscious herding brain could take over and force you to say something you don't believe to keep from being ridiculed.

It takes strong will and conscious focus to be willing to go against the group, and it is even more difficult when those people are like you. So, if these are people you want to impress (or are similar to), you will be more likely to go with the group than trust your gut, again especially at times when you are less confident in yourself.

You know those signs in hotels asking you to reuse your towel? They likely said something about saving the environment by using less water, which is great. When using this tactic, about 35 percent of people will comply and reuse their towels.[92] Not bad.

When herding was incorporated and the signs read, "75 percent of guests reuse their towels, please do so as well," there was a 26 percent increase in towel reuse.

What about when they took it one step further and said, "75 percent of the people who have stayed *in this room* reused their towels."

That may seem like a weird statement, but this slight tweak in messaging—just a few words' difference—was the most effective, with a 33 percent increase in towel reuse. Crazy, huh?

This also works with getting people to use less energy or encouraging people to vote or drive more fuel-efficient vehicles—all sorts of things.[93] Our desire to herd is ingrained in us and is always part of our choices, whether we realize it or not.

Do you remember the TV show *Candid Camera*? They have a video of people facing the wrong way in the elevator.[94] You can watch those who were not in on the experiment looking perplexed and then turning to face the left, right, or back of the elevator instead of facing forward (like normal) to be part of the group. Similarly, if you are walking down the street and see someone looking up at the sky—or better yet, a group of people looking up—chances are, you will stop and look up too.[95]

The Moral

People like to be part of the group. This is increased when they are similar (for example, their friends or neighbors, or people who stayed in the same room) or when they are not confident about their own knowledge (like investment strategies).

Whatever your business does, you are in the business of solving problems. The only reason people buy anything is to solve a problem (whether it is the problem of being hungry or the problem of how to market their business). And problems make people feel anxious or uneasy. That means people are more likely to embrace herding behavior when buying things and to look to see what others like them have done before them. More on that in the next chapter.

Applying Herding

Remember: Humans are a herding species. We constantly seek the approval of the group and rely on others' behavior to shape our own.

Try It Yourself: There are endless places to sprinkle herding cues throughout your messaging: emails, websites, sales conversations, internal communications. List the top five places where you can incorporate herding to make it easier for people to take action (we will work on the messaging for how to do that in the next chapter):

1. _____

2. _____

3. _____

4. _____

5. _____

Bonus Exercise! The biggest eye-opener when it comes to herding is realizing just how often you are doing things just because everyone else is. Be on the lookout for your own herding tendencies so you can spot opportunities to use it in your future business messaging. Here are some examples of how it might be creeping in:

- Why do you feel you need to promote your business on TikTok? Does it align with your specific goals (and where your target market is), or is it because you worry about being judged if you aren't there?

- When do you talk yourself out of trying that new thing (applying for the promotion, starting a podcast, writing a book, emailing that potential client)? What is really keeping you from doing it? Is it a bad idea, or is your subconscious worried about what others will say if you fail?

- Before making that investment or buying into a "can't-lose" new fad, consider whether you (or the person promoting it) did the due diligence. How much is fear of going against the herd impacting your desire to act?

More Herding

Find herding in these chapters: Behavioral Baking (21), The Truth About Pricing (22)

The next chapter on social proof will take herding to the next level. To learn more about how herding works, and specifically how it impacts us when making investments, check out these two episodes of *The Brainy Business* podcast:

- **(Episode 19) Herding: Come On And Listen…Everyone Else Is Doing It.** Learn how to use herding to be more effective on social media, when starting a movement, and understand why things like the Ice Bucket Challenge go viral.

- **(Episode 30) Booms, Bubbles and Busts: Why We Keep Getting Caught Up in the Hype (And How We Can Stop).** Investments through the ages, from tulip bulbs to Beanie Babies and cryptocurrency, it's all here! Learn from the herding fails of the past so you can have a better investment future.

CHAPTER 12

Social Proof

The concept of social proof was first introduced by Robert Cialdini. His 1984 book *Influence: The Psychology of Persuasion* introduced social proof as one of the six principles of persuasion (the others are reciprocity, scarcity, authority, consistency, and liking).[96]

Social proof and herding feel like a bit of a chicken-and-egg situation to me. Because we are a herding species, we look for social proof to validate our decisions and be accepted by the group, but when social proof is present...we are more likely to herd. Which came first? I don't know if this question has an answer, or that it really matters. What *is* important is how these concepts impact your business.

As you know from the last chapter, humans herd like sheep, guppies, and all sorts of other animals. Because of this, when we are presented with a decision or circumstance in which we are uncertain, we look for clues to help us make the best choice.

Seeing a lot of other people have made the same choice in the past (regardless of whether it's good) is the social proof we need to nudge us into making the same choice (more on that in the next chapter).

There are six types of social proof:

- Expert
- Celebrity

- User

- Wisdom of the crowd

- Wisdom of friends

- Certification

Expert

Having an industry expert recommend or speak on behalf of a product or service is very impactful on the brain of your consumer. This could be anything from "four out of five dentists recommend our toothpaste" to the testimonials where someone says, "I'm not only the CEO, I'm also a customer" or when I am a guest on a podcast or speaking about behavioral economics at a conference or corporate training.

Experts extend a halo effect to the organization (present for all types of social proof, not just experts). When you are using a doctor (or anyone in uniform), you also get the benefit of authority bias—essentially, people are more likely to trust someone in a uniform even if they aren't an expert on the subject they're speaking about.

Someone wearing a lab coat giving you stock advice feels more credible than someone in ripped blue jeans, even if the person in blue jeans knows more about the topic. The expert halo from being in authority (a presumably professional person in a lab coat) carries into topics that person doesn't necessarily have expertise in.

This is one reason I recommended that my veterinarian clients who were incorporating telemedicine during the pandemic still wear their lab coats and stethoscopes during video appointments. Logically, it makes no sense. You can't use the stethoscope, and your advice should be interpreted the same way regardless of what you're wearing, or whether you are sitting in your kitchen or in the exam room. However, from what you now know about **priming** and authority bias, wearing the "uniform" can make people more likely to believe you and take your advice seriously.

The gentle reminder that you (or someone you are featuring in your business) are an expert will trigger social proof and help customers feel more comfortable buying from you or believing the claims you make. Just don't overdo it. Much like the ridiculous loss aversion example, if you blast people with a fire hose of expertise claims, it will backfire.

In your business, consider how you might bring in experts to interact with your audience—maybe for a webinar, Facebook Live, Twitter chat, or testimonial.

Celebrity

Similar to an expert statement, having a celebrity endorse your product or service packs a real punch.

And, thankfully, this extends beyond Oprah and the Kardashians. These days, there are microinfluencers on social media who can make a big difference for brands. Microinfluencers have audiences that trust their judgment and recommendations for basically every niche market.

When my brain needs a break, I love to watch videos of people frosting cakes and cookies on Instagram. They are always showcasing a specific brand's piping tips, sprinkle mix, cookie cutter, or food coloring—the opportunities are endless, and these people are celebrities to their followers.

Too often, people in business get swept up in needing to reach as many people as possible. That is not the best strategy. You need to reach the right people in a way that will encourage them to take action.

Think about your business and what you need to reach your goals this year. If you are in a service-based business, it might be only ten more clients, or maybe you want to move from selling 20,000 units to 25,000. Even my corporate clients that move hundreds of millions of product units a year still don't need to have every single person on earth get blasted with whatever they are selling.

Why waste money generically marketing to five million people to try to reach those extra 5,000, when you can target 50,000 who are more likely to buy from their trusted microinfluencer?

It is a smart investment that also helps real people make a difference in their bottom line. I love the idea of microinfluencers, where you know that, for the most part, an investment with them is helping a real family and has real impact.

A word of caution: It is important to be discerning and make sure there is alignment between the celebrity/microinfluencer and your brand (don't just take anyone who is easy or affordable). Research shows[97] that the perceived personality of the celebrity carries over to the perceived personality of the brand and, to have the biggest impact, these two personalities should make sense together (remember how important your brand is from Part I).

In general, it is better to have the right microinfluencer endorsing your brand than it is to have the wrong big-name celebrity.

User

A genuine user talking about the product is influential. This is increased when the person sharing about the product gets no direct benefit (i.e., isn't paid to endorse) and is seen as like those who are looking to buy now. When you can help people see that others like them have found value from your business, it is a win.

Here are some ways you can showcase this type of social proof:

- If you give presentations, sprinkle in phrases like, "Last year, I worked with a client who" or "Someone in my membership group just asked a similar question."

- Know your audience. If you have specific examples from working with customers like them, use these examples. For instance, I have some core presentations I give to groups. The concepts are the same, but when speaking at a financial services conference, I will use examples from banking clients and when speaking at a veterinary conference, there are examples from my vet clients.

- Incorporate lots of testimonials—and don't feel obligated to use them in their totality or attribute them to a specific person. Think of a movie trailer. My speaker sheet and website include lots of quotes like, "Terrific," "Awesome," and "Fantastic." Many were part of longer quotes, but they have a much bigger impact when the key words are separated out.

Wisdom of the Crowd

Let's say someone follows you on Twitter—how would you decide if they are worth following back? You probably check their profile to learn more about them, and followers probably had a big impact on your decision. Your brain's internal dialogue was likely either, "Hmmm…only 500 followers? I don't think so." Or "Wow! 50,000 followers! I better check out what they've got going on!"

That second account may be 49,999 bots and the person's mom, but your brain doesn't know that when it makes the snap decision. You have an immediate instinct that this person is more valuable and worth following than someone with fewer followers.

Similarly, a product on Amazon with 100,000 ratings or a restaurant with more Yelp reviews feels like it must be better than those with fewer. Those buyers might be nothing like you, but your brain sees a large number and thinks, "They must know something I don't" and wants to jump on the train.

If you have a lot of past customers or clients, or downloads of a podcast, or subscribers to your YouTube channel, it is worth sharing.

Those numbers, even shown off to the side, will be noticed.

Other versions of this concept in action include:

- "25 people are looking at this flight to Australia right now"

- "Only 2 left at this price" (a lot of people must be buying it; also triggers scarcity)

- McDonald's "Over 99 billion served" sign

- A Starbucks on every corner (must be popular if there are so many)

When you are looking at sheer volume, that is the "wisdom of the crowd" in action.

Wisdom of Your Friends

When you already know, like, and trust someone who is sharing about a product, service, or brand, it carries more weight than a random user.

One really easy way to use this in your business is via Facebook ads to friends of people who like your page already—then, when the potential liker sees the ad, it will say something like "Melina Palmer and forty-two other friends like this page," which will make that person more likely to consider liking the page too.

You can also ask people to share photos of themselves using your product. Often this is done as part of a contest. Making it easy and fun for people to tag you is great and can help their friends to learn about you, which will make them in turn more likely to want to do business with you as well.

This is one of the most powerful forms of social proof, and yet businesses don't use it enough. When was the last time you asked your customers to recommend you to a friend or family member? No incentives needed, just a simple, "Do you have one friend who is looking for a chiropractor? We had a spot open up next week."

One of my clients, Niche Skincare, produces a high-end restorative serum. To include social proof into their offering when launching the brand, I recommended including a small sample in every box with a simple note card encouraging the customer to "share the love" with a friend or family member. The card included a hashtag and the Niche Instagram handle to help encourage people to post about their sharing.[98] This encourages word-of-mouth referrals and triggers reciprocity (Chapter 20).

Certification

Sometimes certifications come as a literal stamp of approval, like the blue checkmark on Twitter or a "Certified Organic" seal on a product. It could also be an award you have won, or the use of the halo effect to show influential past clients, places you have spoken, or a publication you write for. This could also be the letters after your name to show you invest in your own learning. Or a list of affiliations or accreditations.

This form of social proof helps people feel comfortable with making a decision because it shows someone else did a considerable amount of due diligence (or at least they *assume* that's the case), which can help them have more confidence in making the same choice.

One similar area, which could arguably be its own category (and some say it is), is earned media. This is when you or your business get featured on the local news or quoted in a magazine or are otherwise getting attention that you (theoretically) can't pay for.

If a product is on *Good Morning America* or featured in *Time*, people typically give it more benefit of the doubt than if it was in a paid advertisement.

Yes, You Need to Say It

Our conscious brains often think, "People must know we have customers, I don't need to say it." Studies have shown again and again that this matters to the subconscious buying brain—a lot. Showing that other people have already been there and liked that is incredibly valuable in getting more customers for your business.

Social proof even helped doctors in Australia stop overprescribing antibiotics—the top 30 percent of prescribers received letters saying, for example, "Your prescribing rate is higher than 91 percent of doctors in the region." This simple nudge brought scripts down 13.6 percent in three months—and resulted in 190,000 fewer prescriptions that year.[99]

Applying Social Proof

Remember: Because we herd, knowing other people have bought or used the product/service before makes us more confident in moving forward.

Try It Yourself: Remember those five places you identified where you could use herding in the last chapter? Use them now and identify which type of social proof you can use and an idea of what it might say here:

1. _____

_____

2. _____

_____

3. _____

_____

4. _____

_____

5. _____

_____

More Social Proof

Find social proof in these chapters: Behavioral Baking (21), The Truth About Pricing (22), How to Sell More of the Right Stuff (23), A Series of Small Steps (24), What Problem Are You Solving? (26)

Social proof is important for everyone in business to understand—not just the marketing and sales teams. It is useful in change management and influences decisions in the back office just as it does for customers. Here are two episodes of *The Brainy Business* podcast that will teach more about using social proof in business:

- **(Episode 87) Social Proof: How to Use Herding to Boost Engagement and Sales.** For more detail on the six types of social proof, how they work, and how to apply them.

- **(Episode 106) The Network Effect: How to Leverage the Power of a Group.** Social platforms like Facebook and Uber benefit from increased users. The network effect is different from social proof, but a great complement to it and worth understanding for anyone working with or creating social apps and platforms.

CHAPTER 13

NUDGES and Choice Architecture

The concept of a nudge in behavioral economics is what you might expect: a gentle touch or tap—a way to get attention or help things get back on track. This is built on the work of Richard Thaler, who won the Nobel Prize in economics in 2017 and coauthored *Nudge: Improving Decisions about Health, Wealth, and Happiness* with Harvard professor Cass Sunstein.[100]

One of my favorite examples of nudging comes from the book's early pages:

Assume you gave every kid in the school the funds and ability to order whatever they wanted from the cafeteria—no adults will ever know. What do you expect they will do? Make a beeline for the cookies and ice cream?

In real life, we find that choice is influenced by context. Whatever was at the front of the line was 25 percent more likely to be chosen—and consequently 25 percent *less* likely to be chosen when moved to the end.

Want kids (and adults) to pick carrot sticks instead of French fries? Put one at eye level and the other out of sight (and, as you now know from the chapter on **priming**, out of *smell* as well).

Consider how you might approach cafeteria design given this knowledge.

You could set it up to make the students "best off"—but who defines that? It could be random, but you might be condemning some kids to obesity if they are in the unlucky "dessert first" model. You may say you want to mimic what people would choose on their own, but we now know that doesn't really exist because, as the example demonstrates, choice changes based on the way the options are presented.

What and how you choose is the burden of the choice architect. And while it may be tempting to become an ostrich, not considering the architecture of the choices you are presenting in advance doesn't mean you aren't influencing behavior. You absolutely are. It is just being done without intention and could be making things worse (or better) without you realizing it.

- The way you lay out items in a physical store is choice architecture

- The default options that appear in a search are nudging people toward a choice

- Putting candidates for the election in alphabetical order will have a different outcome from listing them in reverse alphabetical order or by seniority

It all matters. Small details that seem like they *shouldn't* matter (there's that word again) can have a huge impact on behavior and choice.

And, according to Thaler and Sunstein, "A nudge is any aspect of the choice architecture that alters people's behavior in a predictable way without forbidding options or significantly changing their economic incentives. To count as a mere nudge, the intervention must be easy and cheap to avoid. Nudges are not mandates. Putting the fruit at eye level counts as a nudge. Banning junk food does not."

To summarize:

1. Everything matters.

2. There are no neutral options.

3. You cannot avoid being a choice architect—any format will influence the choices, so it is best to be informed and deliberate.

4. Nudges can help simplify complex choices and help illogical humans make good decisions.

5. Nudges are not mandates—they need freedom of choice to count as a nudge.

Choice Architecture

While choice architecture and nudges are very closely tied, they are not the same thing.

A **choice architect** is someone who indirectly influences the choices of other people. This means you set up the mechanism by which others will select their own choice—and the *choice architecture* is the mechanism you select.

A **nudge** is something you would use to influence the decision, in the way the choice architecture is set up, to help the individual trying to make the decision at hand to do the best job possible.

Here's an example:

Imagine you work in HR and have been tasked with boosting enrollment in the retirement plan and encouraging participants to contribute more to get the 10 percent match. We know **status quo bias** plays a factor here; one study found that 86 percent of people who said they planned to change their allocations in the next few months had done nothing four months later.[101] How can you help everyone do what they want and know is in their best interest?

By putting on your choice architecture hat and giving a little nudge.

Perhaps you put together a form that all employees need to complete. (Note: the form is mandatory, a retirement contribution is not).

Presenting Choices

Which comes first? The first item in the list will have the most weight in the brain, so it is best to put the recommendation at the beginning. Is there a default?

What is the question you ask on the form?

Remember, everything matters, including the way you **frame** the question. Consider how you feel compelled to respond to each of the following:

- Regarding a retirement allocation, I would like to: _____

- How much would you like to contribute toward your retirement?

- Experts recommend contributing 15 percent of your salary to a 401(k); how much would you like to allocate?

Do you hear the difference?

Choice architecture and nudges are complex—this example includes framing, priming, anchoring, social proof, and herding, to name a few, and this is just the *question*!

What are the options you include in your choice architecture? How do you word them? Do you simply have two check boxes for "Yes" or "No" and then a line to write in the amount they want to contribute?

What is the default if they do nothing? Do they stay at their individual status quo of no contribution? Or do they get the recommended "expert" opinion and start contributing 15 percent? That could be extreme, and may be unconventional, but it is an option and worth considering (even if it scares your **herding** brain).

Maybe you list the choices as:

- Yes, I want to contribute the recommended 15 percent.

- Yes, I want to contribute, but let's start at 10 percent.

- Yes, I want to contribute at 5 percent.

- Yes, I want to contribute some other amount: _____.

- No, I do not wish to contribute yet.

As you can see, there are many options in wording to help nudge people to contribute higher amounts, but again, it is very easy to opt out and say "no thank you" by checking a different box on the same form.

People still have free choice. They still have all the information (perhaps even more useful information, if you include the recommended contribution being 15 percent—a detail they may not otherwise have).

Proper choice architecture and nudges can increase profitability when used on menus, help people save more for retirement, decrease infection rates and deaths at hospitals, increase organ donations, get more money for public parks, help people use less energy, make cars safer, help you remember to take your card out of the ATM—and so much more.[102]

NUDGES

NUDGES is an acronym created by Thaler and Sunstein to feature the different types and aspects of nudging.[103] They include:

- iNcentives

- Understand Mappings

- Defaults

- Give Feedback

- Expect Error

- Structure Complex Choices

What follows is a brief explanation of each. They are intentionally out of order to make more sense to the brain.

iNcentives

Incentives are more than year-end bonuses. Instead, ask these questions:

- Who uses?

- Who chooses?

- Who pays?

- Who profits?

As you can appreciate, those are not likely the same person/entity, and each question can have multiple answers as the choices get more complex. Our lazy brains don't spend enough time considering who is receiving an incentive beyond ourselves. It is never as simple as "Do you want this? Yes or no."

Good choice architects understand how to structure the nudges to align incentives and accomplish what is best for their business, employees, customers, and greater community. When I did the series on NUDGES on *The Brainy Business* podcast, I gave the example of buying an HVAC unit because we were in the middle of replacing ours. When the guy presented our quote, he asked very offhandedly at the end if we would like a wi-fi-enabled unit and said, "It costs the same, but a lot of people don't want it so…you know…if you want the regular one we can do that too, just let me know what you want."

My response was, "What does the wi-fi-enabled unit do?"

Come to find out, that means we could change the temperature from anywhere, at any time, using an app on the phone. Ever been cold in the middle of the night and didn't want to get out from under your cozy covers to turn on the heat? Solved! A few taps on your phone and the heat is on. As the homeowner, it feels like a clearly better option (especially when there is no difference in price).

This made me wonder about the incentives they have in place, so let's revisit our four questions: who uses, chooses, and pays seems fairly straightforward. This is my husband and me. But who *profits* gets a little more complicated. The easy answer is "the business," but there are likely layers of incentives there. Is it possible that reps receive a smaller commission on the wi-fi-enabled unit?

For the sake of argument, let's assume the company is making everything the same price by taking the difference of a more expensive item out of the rep's commission (perhaps it's a hundred dollars less). He is now incentivized to nudge me (potentially subconsciously) to get the standard unit because it is better for him.

Do you like the idea of having a few hundred icy trips to the thermostat in the middle of the night over the next ten to twenty years because of a hundred dollars in someone else's pocket? Me neither. If the incentives were properly aligned, it could ensure that the customers get the best option because the sales staff are incentivized to promote it. Win-win-win.

Is It Always About Money?

It is important to note that not all incentives are monetary. In fact, nonmonetary incentives often work better than ones with money involved. When Gleb Tsipursky, CEO of Disaster Avoidance Experts, was on the podcast, he shared a project he did for the Edison Welding Institute, which is featured in his book, *Never Go with Your Gut*. The company wanted the engineers to do more marketing—networking, conferences, white papers, blogs, and the like—and they tried all kinds of financial incentives and logical explanations for why it mattered to the company, but to no avail. That's when they brought in Gleb. His research found that the engineers were motivated by social status. So, he recommended the company align the incentives with those emotional motivators. Status-related incentives, like employee of the month, were given to engineers who did the marketing tasks. And the behavior changed.

When Tim Houlihan, founder of Behavior Alchemy, was on the show, he shared a study he did with Dan Ariely on motivating call center employees. Half were given monetary incentives between $60 and $250 and the rest were given nonmonetary incentives equivalent to the cash rewards, including binoculars, slow cookers, and bicycles. Everyone said that cash would be more motivating than merchandise; cash was what they wanted, but the nonmonetary group put in more effort and produced 32 percent more results than the cash group.

Let's revisit the HVAC story with a nonmonetary incentive angle. Maybe he was under-trained and didn't feel comfortable answering questions. Or perhaps the wi-fi-enabled unit has a more tedious paperwork process on the back end that he wanted to avoid.

The question for you to ask is, what is the emotional motivator and how can you align that with the right incentives for the company and your customers?

Defaults

Most people will stick with the default, regardless of what it is.

When the state of Washington started including a five-dollar donation in all vehicle tab renewals, which can easily be removed at the time of payment, they changed the default.

In its first year, the switch raised an additional $1.4 million for the state parks. Pretty impressive for such a small change, don't you think?[104]

That's the power of a well-structured default.

Expect Error and Give Feedback

Brains are busy and they make mistakes. We forget our keys, leave the card in the ATM, drive away without putting the gas cap back on, or forget to put on our seat belt. (This extends beyond driving, of course, but look at how many flubs we might make in a single trip!)

You know how your car dings when you forget to buckle up? That is a feedback nudge put in place because the manufacturers expected you to make an error at some point.

Make a list of every place where your customers might err. What nudge can you put in place? What complimentary products and services could you create to solve these problems? How can you anticipate the errors to help them feel better about their choices?

Yes, it truly is that simple. However, it is important to choose your feedback wisely. If your car dinged and beeped and had lights flashing at you for every little thing, it would become too much; you'd start to ignore the alerts, so none of them would have any impact.

Giving feedback is more than beeps and lights. Here are some of my favorite examples:

- Glidden's special ceiling paint that goes on bright pink and dries white to ensure coverage.[105]

- Strategically painted lines around a dangerous curve in Chicago, which get closer together as you approach the turn, making your brain think you are speeding up. This simple nudge reduced crashes by 36 percent.[106]

- The click sound when you take a picture on your phone. That isn't part of its functionality, but it reduces people saying, "Did it take it?" so they have a better experience.

- A clicked website link changes color and the pinwheel turns while the Mac is thinking for these same reasons—they keep you from clicking sixty-five times to ensure it is working (and inadvertently making everything slower).

- Nissan's eco pedal is harder to press down when you are burning a lot of fuel, making your driving greener.[107]

Helping people to know they are on the right path by providing them with a little feedback nudge goes a long way in overall experience.

Understanding Mapping to Structure Complex Choices

Some tasks—like picking out an ice cream flavor—are relatively easy, while others—like choosing a place to live—are considerably more complex. But at their core, they are both built on the foundation of a mapping, which Thaler and Sunstein explain as a path from the choice to its outcome.

With ice cream, most people know what flavor they might choose—especially if there are only three flavors: do you want strawberry, chocolate, or vanilla? You have a favorite, and some sort of mapping in your brain already letting you know which choice you will enjoy most. And, if they have considerably more flavors—maybe some exotic ones you have never tried before, like lemon lavender or maple bacon—you can always do a taste test to see which you like best and avoid accidentally buying a giant scoop of ice cream that tastes more like soap than something scrumptious.

But what about something more complex, like an apartment search? The mapping from choice to outcome (your "welfare" as Thaler and Sunstein call it) is much more difficult to see. Even if there are still only three options to choose from, there are a lot of variables to consider, including price, location, commute, size, neighbors, and furnishings.

It is the task of any choice architect to set up a system that makes the map clear and easy to use so the chooser can select the best option for them. I've created a five-step process to incorporate this into your business:

1. Encourage thoughtful review and open-mindedness.

2. Break it down.

3. Make it relatable.

4. Help them get there.

5. Call to action.

1. Encourage Thoughtful Review and Open-Mindedness

For big decisions, it is important to understand your biases and theirs when mapping out the choice architecture. What can you do to incorporate thoughtful review and an open mind (for both you and the chooser)?

This step is not as important in trivial decisions, but it can still be helpful. Consider the flavors of ice cream. It is not life or death, but if you have seventy-five flavors available and they all have weird names like "Phish Food" or "Chunky Monkey," what are you doing to help the potential customer be open-minded and try something new? What do they need to know and how can you relate back to their existing maps?

2. Break It Down

If you want to make a map, it is important to understand all the options someone has available.

What are they considering, what is their mental state, and what should they be aware of to help them make the best choice? This is a big chunk of where you should spend your planning time in building the map. Thaler, Sunstein, and Balz[108] give a great example using cameras that I found amazingly relatable, so let's use that.

Imagine you work at Nikon. Your customer's choice is not just, do they want a Coolpix or a DSLR model, but do they need a camera apart from the one on their phone? Or do they want to buy an Olympus or a Canon? Should they get something with video capabilities? And how many megapixels should they get? Should they just rent a camera when they need one? Maybe get disposable cameras when they travel? It becomes a very daunting choice very quickly.

Breaking the problem into its components can help you create the map, which will in turn help you anticipate questions and guide them to the right recommendation. You are the expert, and they want to know they are making a good choice. Something they will be happy with. Breaking it down will help you get them there, and then...

3. Make It Relatable

Use the components from the last step and think about how it relates to someone with no knowledge of your industry jargon. In the camera world, we have the issue of the megapixel. Customers tend to think bigger is better—that's natural—but what do I get if I go from seven to eight megapixels? Or ten? Or a thousand, for that matter? Most non-professionals have no idea what the difference is, other than a larger file size (which will result in a worse experience).

How can you make it relatable?

What if instead you ditched "megapixels" and cameras were listed as: web-only, four-by-six print, poster-size, and billboard? I know I will never need images so crisp they could be blown up to the size of a billboard. But I might take a photo so great I would like to hang it on my wall, so poster-size it is. Easy. The new concept and relatable mapping made it easier for me to make the decision—and it is something I feel good about.

What sorts of things that are obvious to you are necessary for your potential client to decide? If you take a step back, what does their subconscious need to know or hear? What rule of thumb will make the choice simple and easy?

Once you have addressed those questions, it is time for step four.

4. Help Them Get There

Once you know what your customers need to make the decision and you have made the choices relatable, your customers still may need a little sample to nudge them over the edge. Using the camera example again, this could be as simple as letting them take some pictures and print them out. Going back to the Phish Food ice cream, you can give a taste test. Building on the last chapter on **social proof**, including a well-placed testimonial can "help them get there" as well.

5. Call to Action

It may seem like someone should know when they are ready to buy, but it often doesn't work that way.

When you are dealing with complex choices, there are often many variables to consider, which can make it confusing. For this reason, it is a good idea to ask people periodically if they are ready to buy or have a "buy now" button.

This presents a stopping point where the customer's brain will think, "Hmmm…do I have enough information yet?" The **primed** implication is that other people typically buy at this stage (**herding**) to help them feel more comfortable with the decision if they do choose to buy.

Wrapping It Up

We humans make an average of 35,000 decisions every day.[109] Most are made using the rules of the subconscious brain—rules you are learning about in this book. Understanding and working with those rules means your customers will find it easier to do business with you, choose the best options for their situation, and be happier about their decisions (which you'll learn more about in Chapter 24).

Customers make countless choices in their interactions with you. And remember, whether you think about the architecture in advance or not, you are still influencing their choices with the way you present the information. So, it is important to think through the incentives, defaults, errors, feedback options, maps, and complex choices so you can nudge customers to make those best possible choices.

Applying NUDGES and Choice Architecture

Remember: You are a choice architect whether you realize it or not—use NUDGES to get the win-wins for your business and its customers.

Try It Yourself: Start simple as you practice nudging. Yes, it can be used for very complex situations, but some of the best nudges are little things, like the light that comes on when you need to replace the filter on your fridge. I recommend starting with the "expect error/give feedback" nudges. Make a list of all the places where your customers are likely to err and possible nudges to help get them back on track (consider all the senses as they are a direct line to the subconscious brain):

What error do you expect? _____

_____

What nudge could you use? _____

_____

What would another nudge look like? _____

_____

What could a nudge sound like? _____

_____

What might a nudge smell like? _____

_____

What other nudges could you use? _____

_____

More NUDGES

Find NUDGES and choice architecture in these chapters: How to Sell More of the Right Stuff (23), A Series of Small Steps (24), May I Take Your Order? (25), What Problem Are You Solving? (26)

Nudging and choice architecture have so many applications and fascinating examples. To learn more, I highly recommend the book *Nudge*, which is cited throughout the chapter. I also did a full, seven-part series on NUDGES and choice architecture on *The Brainy Business* podcast that will teach more about using them in business:

- **(Episodes 35–41) NUDGES and Choice Architecture: A Seven-Part Series.** An introductory episode followed by up to an hour on each aspect of NUDGES: iNcentives, Understand Mapping, Defaults, Give Feedback, Expect Error, Structure Complex Choices.

- **(Episode 109) Secrets of Motivation and Incentives, with Tim Houlihan.** So many amazing insights about what really motivates people and how to incentivize them. Tim is also the cohost of the *Behavioral Grooves* podcast, of which I was a guest on their episode 109 as well!

- **(Episode 111) Avoiding Everyday Work Disasters, with Gleb Tsipursky.** Got a big decision you don't want to screw up? Use Gleb's five-step process shared in this episode.

CHAPTER 14

Paradox of Choice

It's Saturday morning and you're meeting a friend for breakfast. After sitting down, you order toast and the waitress says, "We have three kinds of spread, would you like grape, strawberry, or orange marmalade?"

You can quickly make a choice—maybe one of those options made you say, "yuck" inside your head immediately, or you know strawberry is your favorite. Either way, you can pretty quickly choose, and this is a simple decision (an easy mapping, to use the language from the last chapter).

What if instead the response was, "Great! We specialize in spreads here, so you just let me know which one you want. We have raspberry, sugar-free raspberry, raspberry vanilla, orange currant, strawberry, triple berry, seedless strawberry, strawberry balsamic, grape, grape lavender, lemon lavender, chocolate, chocolate hazelnut, marionberry, blackberry breeze, cinnamon sugar, peanut butter, almond butter, maple mango, or pineapple."

You would likely be left feeling dumbfounded. This is now an extraordinarily complex choice. Do you want savory or sweet? Seedless or sugar-free? What in the world would maple mango taste like? Did they say grape lavender? How much sugar is in the cinnamon sugar...and is that a spread or a sprinkle? Is the peanut butter chunky or smooth?

You might instead say, "Forget it. I'll just have coffee."

The entire experience with the restaurant is now tainted with frustration. Breaking this offering into groupings could have made a difference (fruit, chocolate, savory) so the choice isn't a hodgepodge of stress for a quickly overwhelmed brain.

Overwhelmed Brain

And just how easily do our brains get overwhelmed? It takes a lot less than you think.

A study in the *Journal of Consumer Research*[110] found that remembering a few extra digits can impact decision-making. One group was given a two-digit number and the other a seven-digit number to remember while going through a series of tasks. One of the tasks was to choose their snack for after the study was over. Those remembering the simpler number were more likely to choose the healthy fruit salad. Those remembering only *five more digits* were more likely to choose chocolate cake.

How often are you heaping mountains of decisions, facts, and figures on your current or potential customers in an attempt to help them make a better choice? Are you ever asking them to remember more than five digits of information and consider multiple things at once? You are likely overwhelming their brain and making the whole experience worse than it has to be.

Time Pressure

Another way our brains get overwhelmed is when our time to act is limited.

Time pressure floods your brain with chemicals that get it a little overwhelmed and feeling like you need to act *right now* so you don't make a mistake and miss out (FOMO).[111] The value doesn't need to be great; it is all about taking an action before the time runs out.

With unlimited time, you are calmer, giving the conscious time to think, process, and evaluate before deciding. But time pressure? Move over, conscious! You're too slow and I've got this down.

Efficient, perhaps. Effective? Not always.

It likely won't surprise you to know that time pressure is a form of stress. You've felt it—you know the anxiety that comes from buying concert tickets and having the little clock on the Ticketmaster website counting down second by second while you fumble to get your credit card.

You feel anxious, worried, and stressed. Your hands might be shaking as you try to read the card, impulsively checking the numbers four or five times before you hit "buy" and then muttering, "Come on…come on…" under your breath while the page loads.

No little clock tick-tick-ticking down? It's magically an easier buying experience.

Holiday Consumption

On average, consumers take several visits to websites before they make a purchase decision, and then, they get an average of 1.2 items. During the holidays? They are more likely to only spend one visit and get an average of 3.5![112] This can be due to the custom of buying gifts for others, which may be outside the norm of how we would act the rest of the year, but it is also influenced by time pressure.

How many daily deals and limited quantities and shopping cart clocks are influencing our decisions at holiday time (which is magnified by the overwhelm of the rest of the holiday experience)?

Holiday parties to plan for! Prepping for families to visit! Gifts to buy (and wrap and deliver or drop in the mail)! The brain is obviously overwhelmed, and overwhelmed brains make worse decisions. Applying time pressure reverses the way we evaluate choices.

Lots of Time = Risk-Averse

Time Pressure = Loss-Averse

People tend to be risk-averse when they have plenty of time available.[113] We don't want to make the wrong choice, so we evaluate the risks of making a decision. But, when time pressure is applied, we become very loss-averse—and then the FOMO takes over.

Time pressure can encourage people to buy an extra item or get something "just in case," especially when paired with a discount, great return policy, or benefit.

Working on a Deadline

Many of us believe we "work better on a deadline"—but is it true? It turns out people are less creative under time constraints.[114] This isn't all that surprising when you think about it. While you may be more focused in the moment and physically completing the task at hand, that doesn't mean the work is better than it would have been if you had accomplished a little at a time when the clock wasn't ticking in your face.

When you think about your brand and strategy work, consider how much value there would be in your brain being as creative as it can be. When doing big-picture planning and setting goals (the stuff you will be doing when you are applying what you learn from this book), it is best to have a calm mind without the pressure of time. Setting aside dedicated time to relax and think can make a big difference.

Ever get ideas while falling asleep, taking a shower, or when out for a run? It's because your brain can relax a little, relieve that pressure, and think more creatively—you can manufacture that and build it into your day by planning time for mind wandering.[115]

Counterintuitively Reducing Call Times

Richard Chataway, CEO of BVA Nudge Unit UK and author of *The Behaviour Business*, shared a story with me about a project with a large savings bank (over twenty million customers).[116]

The bank was looking to reduce the length of calls coming into their customer service department to save money while increasing efficiency and satisfaction. One of the things Richard and his team found in their research was that getting people to properly answer a security question (one of the first hurdles to clear) was causing a lot of unnecessary problems. Staff inadvertently set customers up to fail by overwhelming their brains, which triggered a much more time-consuming and difficult process to do business.

The first point of overwhelm was saying "If you fail this question, we can't help you." That phrasing creates a lot of stress on the brain. A simple reframe of "When you correctly answer this question, we can move on to solve your problem" relieved that pressure, setting them on the road to success.

When the BVA team went on to recommend the staff say, "Take your time" after asking the security question, the bank was hesitant. It may seem counterintuitive when you already have long call times to actively tell people to take their time when coming up with an answer. But people were more likely to correctly answer the question when told to take their time— relieving the time pressure and overwhelm in the brain. Taking a few extra moments to correctly answer the first question saved oodles of frustration and time down the line. Satisfaction went up for customers and staff, while also reducing the average call length by 11 percent. For a company of their size, that could mean millions each year—all from a simple reduction in brain pressure and overwhelm.

As you look to apply the behavioral concepts you learn in this book, always keep overwhelm and brain stress at the core of your process. Roger Dooley gives fantastic examples of ways to reduce this in his book *Friction*, which we discussed on episode 72.[117] You will be amazed at how many points of friction are causing overwhelm in your business, from expense reports to your website. Reducing overwhelm in the brain by applying behavioral nudges and other tools from this book can do wonders in your conversion and satisfaction scores.

Small Steps

When I help clients with reducing overwhelm to make the buying process easier, we start by identifying the small steps in the process. These are the microdecisions everyone needs to go through to choose to buy from you.

Often, people are looking at the experience as "we send the email/direct mail piece/online ad and then they buy"—but there are many little steps along the way in that process. Consider an ad on social media:

- Be on the social channel.

- Algorithm determines it should be in their feed.

- It is interesting enough that they notice it and stop.

- Read headline and continue to be interested enough to glance at the shortened text.

- Care enough to click "see more" and continue reading.

- Read enough to understand the call to action.

- Choose to leave the social channel (full of brain rewards) to do the action now.

- Once on that page, remain compelled enough to find what they are supposed to do (let's say it is complete a form).

- Have that form be easy enough to complete to get through quickly (each box is a step).

- Hit send or submit.

When you are working with an easily distracted brain that is evaluating eleven million bits of information per second, it is critical to consider all these points in the process—even for something as simple as a Facebook ad (or website landing page, email blast, advertisement, or direct mailer).

Chapter 24 is dedicated to my "Series of Small Steps" approach, but I want you to be primed with this idea now as you go through the next several chapters.

Reducing the Paradox of Choice

Remember: The human brain is overwhelmed very easily. Reduce friction, time pressure, unnecessary choices, and stress to improve the experience and satisfaction of your customers and employees.

Try It Yourself: Look at your buying process:

- How many choices and microdecisions are there?

- Is it well-structured and easy for someone to choose? Or are you bombarding them with fifty kinds of jam?

- What do people need to know in each moment?

- What can they learn later?

- What pieces are there for your team's benefit, but making it harder on the customer?

- What would a streamlined, frictionless experience be?

Pro Tip: Instead of looking for places to trim down what exists, step away and consider what the simplest version would look like. For example, when working through a website experience for a client, I never let them have the existing website up when we are discussing what the new site needs. The new simplified experience should be unencumbered by **status quo bias** and **loss aversion** toward what already exists.

More Paradox of Choice

Find paradox of choice in these chapters: A Series of Small Steps (24), May I Take Your Order? (25), What Problem Are You Solving? (26)

I don't think I've ever seen a business that couldn't benefit from a little less friction. Even when customers tell you they want lots more choices, it will likely be a barrier that keeps them stuck, so be wary of too many options and details. Expand your knowledge with these episodes of *The Brainy Business* podcast:

- **(Episode 32) The Overwhelmed Brain and Its Impact on Decision-Making.** More details on the chocolate cake study, and my tips for overcoming overwhelm.

- **(Episode 72) Friction: What It Is and How to Reduce It.** An interview with Roger Dooley about his fantastic book and how to reduce friction in your business.

- **(Episode 74) Time Pressure: The Stress of a Ticking Clock.** How time pressure is different from scarcity and loss aversion and how to use it in business.

- **(Episode 134) How to Apply Behavioral Science for Business Success.** An interview with Richard Chataway with many amazing examples of using behavioral economics in business.

CHAPTER 15

Partitioning

Friday night. You're about to settle in for a binge-watching session on Netflix and it's time to choose your snack. The pantry has one unopened party-sized bag of Cheetos and about ten of those fun-sized bags. Which do you choose?

If you opted for the single, big bag, you will eat more than if you were to go with the individualized bags—even if you brought them all out to the couch with you.

When something is partitioned into smaller containers and you are required to take an action to get more (grab and open another bag or box), it creates a new decision point—a small transaction cost—and will drastically reduce the number of people who tear into another serving and keep eating.[118]

It is much easier to continue reaching into the open bag of Cheetos; you already made the decision to open the bag and eat them, and each reach into the bag is just supporting the decision you made earlier. To your brain, it feels like it is part of the same decision to "eat chips," and serving size kind of goes out the window until you hit a barrier (i.e., bottom of bag or stomachache).

How do you know when you are "full?"

Multiple studies over many years have proven that the feeling in your stomach isn't the best gauge. In one example, people who were given larger servings of macaroni and cheese ate 27 percent more—but the amount consumed didn't impact how full people felt.[119] Another study found that adding horizontal lines on large cups,[120] which served as a measurement reminder so people drinking could see how much they were drinking, reduced consumption.

Clearly, fullness and serving size are triggered by our eyes more than our stomachs.

Decision-making opportunities (open a new bag, see lines on a cup, ask for a refill) increase awareness and the amount of cognitive processing used. Whether you think of this from the aspect of a business or as a consumer, this can be both good and bad.

In some cases, you want to *eliminate* the choice, because stopping to think about the decision over and over may result in someone changing their mind. Imagine if Netflix asked if you wanted to maintain your subscription and you had to opt back in every month. They would have a lot fewer subscribers, but it doesn't necessarily mean anyone would be happier about it.

Other times, you want to infuse *more* choices to get the benefit of partitioning. Beyond mindless eating or spending, a business could use the same logic to help employees think more creatively. Maybe a notification that pops up a few times daily, encouraging them to walk around and contemplate a random business problem. This partition can help employees to use their brains differently throughout the day and consider various ways to make the company better. Win-win.

Even seemingly insignificant changes can trigger partitioning. All it needs to do is get the person to stop and think—even for just a second. But beware, the effect can diminish over time.

You know that little white paper between cookies in a package?[121]

The white paper has become so common it doesn't reduce consumption. Though participants took longer to eat the cookies than those with no partitions, 94 percent still finished them all. But when partitions of different colors were introduced between the twenty-cookie stacks? Participants ate slower and only 22 percent finished all the cookies!

Effort matters, but drawing the attention of the conscious brain does too.[122]

Beyond Food

Partitioning impacts more than our mouths and stomachs; it also has a big impact on units of money. In this study, participants were given envelopes with a total of a hundred coupons to gamble with.[123] No one had to gamble; they could have cashed in their coupons for a few bucks, and everyone had the option to cash in at any time. Here's how the groups were split:

- One envelope with a hundred coupons

- Four envelopes of twenty-five coupons each

- Ten envelopes with ten coupons each

It probably won't surprise you to learn that, once an envelope was opened, all its coupons were destined for the casino. That being said, it probably didn't shake down the way you think.

Those most likely to spend nothing were in the single-envelope category, but those who did open tended to leave with no coupons left. People in the ten-envelope category opened the most envelopes, but never more than four. And those in the four-envelope group had most people stop at three, but that means they still gambled considerably more than the ten-envelope group:

- Opening four of ten envelopes = forty coupons gambled

- Opening three of four envelopes = seventy-five coupons gambled

Can you see how easy it is to be tricked by your brain and think you are doing good by "only opening three" but not realizing that, if the coupons had been segmented differently, you would have spent a lot less? And again, you likely wouldn't even realize the difference, and would feel just as good about yourself having had restraint and only gambling seventy-five of your hundred coupons as if you had opened half of the envelopes in the ten-envelope group.

OPEN 4 OF 10 ENVELOPES

OPEN 3 OF 4 ENVELOPES

=

=

40

75

COUPONS GAMBLED

COUPONS GAMBLED

The number of envelopes opened can trick your brain into gambling more.

And remember, nothing was stopping you or forcing you to keep going in these scenarios. There is no reason anyone in the single-envelope group couldn't have stopped at twenty-five, fifty, or seventy-two coupons, but they were much less likely to do so without the teeny-tiny transaction cost, the split second to think, from having the coupons in a new envelope.

Partitioning money has also been found to help people save more or spend less. One study in rural China and India found that workers who received their payments in four sealed envelopes saved more than those who received their pay in a single bundle.[124]

This is known as the **shopping momentum effect**.[125] Essentially, once you start the process of spending, you are more likely to spend again until you hit a partition.

This partition can involve having to break large bills, but it can also involve moving into a second mental account (from checking to savings, debit to credit card, or to a second credit card).

This is why stores will make an effort to get people in with a loss leader, because once you have made the transition from "just browsing" to "buying," you will likely be in that mode until you hit a new partition or barrier. And there are some really cool studies that show you don't even have to be physically buying, but just thinking in the right way about buying can make someone transition into the new mode and be more likely to buy unrelated items.[126]

Using Partitions in Business

Partitioning is impactful on more than eating, spending, and physical barriers. Any cognitive intervention—something that makes the user stop and think—can trigger partitioning (for better or worse). This can be done using sound, rhetorical questions, targets, or progress markers.

Sound: What if, instead of having your air conditioning set to the same temperature all day long, it turned off every few hours and made a *ding* so you could decide if and when to turn it back on? Being forced to physically get up and turn it on might nudge you to wait a couple hours and use less energy.

Rhetorical Questions: Once, in the Portland airport, my husband and I decided to buy a big bag of almonds before our long travel day. We buy enough almonds to know that they were a little more expensive than at our grocery store, but not astronomically priced for an airport. After handing our items to the cashier, she held out the almonds and said, "Are you aware how much these cost?"

We looked at each other, shrugged and said, "Ummm...I think so?" to which she said, "They're $12.99. Are you *sure* you want to buy them?" (Cue extreme facial expression.)

Feeling shamed by our potentially extravagant almond purchase, we decided not to buy them—even though we wanted them and had no problem with the price. Her bringing it up and forcing us to rethink our decision caused anticipated regret and significantly lowered the total amount we spent there. It doesn't mean anything to her as the cashier, I'm sure, but the business probably isn't happy with that.

Though this is a great example of how looking at the wrong metrics can negatively impact your business.

The cashier probably did this because a lot of people would buy a big bag of almonds and then complain about how expensive it was, causing returns. Maybe the company told the cashiers to confirm with everyone that they knew the price before purchasing almonds. This has now caused a negative spiral where they ask in a way that creates a partition and rethinking of the purchase, which means they sell less almonds. The cashiers may even report and say, "Yup, we knew it! So many people put back the bags of almonds after they heard the price. We saved so many returns!"

What they likely did was unnecessarily stop purchases from customers who would have been satisfied with their decision to buy almonds—and now feel a little worse about themselves after the interaction at the business. This is an example of a lose-lose situation, where adding a partition is worse for everyone involved.

It's easy to talk people out of a sale or make them feel bad about a purchase (or start to regret it), even when you are trying to be helpful.

Continually asking, "Are you sure?" creates unnecessary partitions. Everyone will eventually say, "I guess not." When someone decides to buy—stop. It's done. You did it. If they have regrets, they can come back, but that's their job, not yours—especially not before the transaction has taken place.

Targets and Progress Markers: Consider the milestone moments in the future that can serve as a partition point, and set check-ins up in advance. For example, if a prospect can't afford to hire you now, you could say, "No problem. Many of my clients budget in August; may I check back then as you identify next year's priorities?"

Building on the examples from the **paradox of choice**, you now know that every step you put back on the prospect is a partition—a point for them to reconsider or forget. In the selling process, this can be as simple as one too many back-and-forth emails. It is your job as the person selling an item (whatever that may be) to make it as easy as possible to do business with you. Consider every person you have ever met at a conference or networking event. How many people were you genuinely interested in working with, but then got too busy to follow up (and felt a little sheepish reaching out six months later, so it was easier to move on to a competitor)?

When that person handed you their card, they probably said something like, "Call me when you're ready" or "Here, go check out our website and let me know if you have any questions." That is an unnecessary partition that made it harder to work with them.

As Nikki Rausch, CEO of Sales Maven, says, instead of handing someone your card and saying, "Call me when you're ready," say, "Let's go ahead and schedule a circle-back call now. How does Wednesday look for you?" This places an important partition—a prescheduled call on their calendar— which they are much more likely to keep than if you call them to follow up unannounced.

Shipping Costs: Recently, I tried to buy a razor holder from a small business's website. The item in question was $6.99 and I wanted it because it would solve a problem for me. I clicked buy—and saw there was an additional shipping fee of $3.99. This item is tiny and can't weigh more than a couple of ounces; it could easily ship in a regular envelope with a couple of stamps. I spent nearly *three weeks* agonizing over whether or not I should buy this thing, revisiting the site and viewing the cart, debating whether I should find it on Amazon, and even asking my husband if he thought it was worth it.

Here's the thing: if it was $9.99 with free shipping, I would have bought it immediately (and excitedly awaited its arrival). Now, the entire brand and experience is tainted by this partition.

Whenever possible, include all the fees (shipping, handling, transaction) in the overall price—even for heavy items. One of my clients sold weighted blankets and had great success with free shipping. People are more excited about free shipping than they are about the difference in the cost of the item. And, no, I don't recommend one-dollar shipping for this reason. If you can do it for a buck, you can do it free.

Applying Partitioning

Remember: Make it easy for people to do business with you. Remove unnecessary partitions in the process and everyone will be happier.

Try It Yourself: Look at every step of your buying process—how many of those points are really necessary? Is there a partition or extra step you can remove? If you have an intake form that people fill out to schedule a call to learn more, how many fields are there (and how many are "required")? How many are *actually* required to do the task at hand?

Remove anything that isn't absolutely necessary to complete this step and you'll be amazed at how many more leads you get in the door. (This, of course, works for product businesses as well. Follow the same steps to find unnecessary partitions, like shipping fees and extra boxes to fill out. What can you remove?)

More Partitioning

Look for partitioning in this chapter: A Series of Small Steps (24)

Learn more about partitioning and making it easy to do business with you on these three episodes of *The Brainy Business* podcast:

- **(Episode 56) Mental Accounting: How to Make Your Money Math Work for You.** There was a brief mention of mental accounting in this chapter; if you want to learn more, check out this full episode on the concept.

- **(Episode 58) Partitioning: Why We Eat More Cheetos from a Party-Sized Bag.** For more studies and tips for applying partitioning in your business.

- **(Episode 96) How to Make It Easy to Do Business with You.** An interview with neuro-linguistic programming expert Nikki Rausch.

CHAPTER 16

Pain of Paying

Eighteen years before Kim Kardashian "broke the internet," AOL beat her to the punch by launching their new pricing model in 1996.[127] Before that, you bought set blocks of internet time:

- Twenty hours a month for $19.95

- Five hours a month for $9.95

Most people chose the twenty-hour model and were using between ten and fifteen hours a month. I'm sure someone at AOL said something like, "You know, 'unlimited' sounds so great. We could put that in our ads and reduce our tracking needs. It could be a win-win!" They probably assumed most people would still stay under twenty hours so it wouldn't be that big of a deal.

After all, someone using ten hours still had plenty of room before hitting their twenty-hour limit, so they must only have ten to fifteen hours' worth of stuff to do, right?

Totally logical. And totally wrong.

Usage quadrupled basically overnight, and AOL couldn't keep up. There were service issues and all sorts of problems—the company was even sued by a few users who struggled to use the system.

What happened? Why did everyone go bonkers once their internet access became unlimited?

Apparently, there was a little meter running in the corner whenever you logged on. You may remember it if you were using AOL about twenty-five years ago, but it was constantly tick-tick-ticking and counting the amount of time you were spending online. This kept the time you were spending in front of your conscious brain (**time pressure**), constantly reminding you there was a point soon where you might go over your limit.

No time limit = no clock.

And we all know how easy it is to get sucked into internet rabbit holes and not realize how long you have been jumping from site to site. Without a giant clock to remind you of the pain you will feel if you go over your limit, you are free to surf as much as you want. AOL learned that lesson the hard way.

This is also why Uber is so much easier to use than traditional taxis, where you are watching the meter tick up while sitting in traffic. Think about how your buying/user experience would differ if:

- Gyms charged for minutes in the facility or number of steps taken.

- Restaurants charged you per bite instead of for the meal.

- Netflix had a clock running and charged you for each fifteen-minute increment or show watched.

Constantly reminding your customers of payments and price is generally a bad business model. There is a very real pain of paying experience— studies show the insula (a pain center in the brain) lights up when making a payment.[128] For us humans, this emotional pain is like physical pain. Luckily, just as Uber and AOL have discovered, there are ways to help people feel less pain when paying for things.

Interestingly, when the payment being made is *time* and not money (for instance, a long wait time), the reverse is true. Telling people about the process and what is going on behind the scenes can make wait times more tolerable. This is why Domino's has the Pizza Tracker; FedEx, UPS, and Amazon give shipping updates; and why Uber's Express POOL service, which has more steps and a longer wait time, built in options to read about how wait times are calculated or showing the process in real time. The knowledge makes the wait time more tolerable.[129]

Context is incredibly important when it comes to the pain caused by making a monetary payment. Consider these two scenarios:

- You've lived in your home for ten years and the carpet is looking a bit dingy, so you get a quote. Replacing the living room's flooring with the same carpet you have now will be $2,500.

- You've had your eye on a beautiful, handwoven rug for months and finally decide to buy it and spruce up your living room. It's a splurge at $2,500, but you love the way it looks.

Why do the two experiences feel different? Does pulling out your credit card to replace the carpet with a newer version cause pain, while buying the designer rug is a rush of adrenaline and excitement?

Both are carpet—coverings on the floor that people will step on—but the way someone feels about the purchase will impact their buying behavior. It is important to know this context when you think about your buying experience. Some important continuums[130] to consider include:

- Is it an investment (appreciating value) or a consumable (depreciating value)?

- How long will they enjoy the benefits?

- How long will it last?

- How visible is the reward?

- How easy is it to justify the expense to other people?

- Is it a routine payment (necessity) or a luxury buy?

- Is it a gift?

- Is the payment made before or after consuming the item?

- Is this the only payment needed to take care of the problem, or will it be drawn out over more?

- What is the motivation and story of the seller?

The handwoven rug is a luxury investment, which you expect to appreciate over time (and if you ever move, you can take it with you). It is expected to last for a long time, and you can enjoy the benefits each day because you love the look of it. This makes the reward visible and easy to justify to others: "I know it was a bit extravagant—but just *look* at it!" You can tell a story in your mind about who is hand-weaving this rug—perhaps you are supporting a solopreneur.

In the case of the carpet, you already know how dingy this thing is going to look in a few years—all you have to look forward to is depreciation. You can't take it with you if you move, and anyone who comes over probably won't notice you replaced it. If you bought from a large company, you won't have the same association with the business and may even question their motivation: "I mean, come on—$2,500 to get the same exact carpet? It's highway robbery! I bet they marked that way up."

Paying and consuming have sort of a reciprocal relationship, because making a payment reduces the joy of consumption, but consumption reduces the pain of paying. When the pain is completely separated from the gain, you feel one much more than the other, or feel each one distinctly as it is experienced.

For example, when you pay with a credit card, the pain is removed. All you have is the joy of getting a new toy—until the bill comes. Then it's all pain (and pain without the gain can be excruciating).

Pay Now or Later?

Great news—you're going on vacation! Choose your experience:

- **Scenario One:** You pay for the entire trip before you go and enjoy margaritas on the beach at your all-inclusive hotel. The excursions, hotel, and flights are all prepaid, so you can just relax and recharge.

- **Scenario Two:** You go on your trip and have all the same excursions, hotel, flights—the same number of margaritas—but it will all be tallied at the end, so you receive a bill two months after returning home. All the joy is gone (the relaxation has completely worn off) and now you're stressed and cursing your past self for going on that extra outing.

In general, luxury items, experiences, and events feel even better when paid in advance. Getting the pain of paying out of the way before the experience starts means you can have all the joy of the gain without any of the dreaded payment pain. And paying in advance is not quite as painful because you have the anticipation of the upcoming trip—the fun you will have once you get there. After the fact, the fun doesn't feel like it was worth the amount you are paying now.

In contrast, if you have a big-ticket item that people will get a lot of value out of over time (house, car, washing machine), making payments while enjoying the item works well. People generally don't mind paying the mortgage each month because they are living in the house each day. If they could only get into a house if they paid the full sum in advance...a lot less people would own homes.

Tightwads and Spendthrifts

While the bulk of the population (about 60 percent) are unconflicted spenders, there are two other groups that are important to keep in mind: tightwads and spendthrifts.[131] Tightwads make up about 25 percent of the population. The pain of paying is too much for them—so they don't buy things they need or would want because it is too difficult to give up money.

> Being a tightwad is not the same as being frugal because they have different motivations. Frugal people are seeking the joy of saving money, and it can be about the hunt of a great deal—tightwads are avoiding the pain in a payment. Someone might be both frugal and a tightwad, but they are not the same.

Opposite to tightwads are people who spend too much, too easily, and do not feel an appropriate amount of pain before or during the spending process; they are called spendthrifts (and they make up the remaining 15 percent).

There are some simple framing shifts, like saying there is a "small five-dollar fee" (instead of just a "five-dollar fee") that make it feel easier for everyone to buy. Also, pointing out how something is an investment can reduce the pain of paying for a tightwad (without having a negative impact on the other two groups). These reframes can help a tightwad feel better about their purchase (less stressed and conflicted) and can actually make them happier with their purchase in the long run.

Another tactic that works well on everyone is to pull the currency out of the equation altogether.

Tokens, Chips, and Gifts

Our brains become accustomed to our own currency over time. We Americans know what a dollar, quarter, dime, nickel, and penny are worth intuitively, so our pain in paying is instinctual. When traveling abroad and using euros, yen, or pounds, it feels a little like play money. It is easier to spend and doesn't feel as painful.[132]

Removing dollar signs and commas helps a number seem smaller and don't trigger the same amount of pain of paying.[133] This is a form of **framing** and can make a difference in buying decisions. Look at the following and see how they feel different:

- $4,272.00

- $4,272

- $4272

- 4272

Converting currency to chips or tokens (like a casino) will make them easier to spend than the money they represent.

And, if you can ever position your product or service as a gift, people are happier spending more—it makes them feel good.[134] Say I've got my eye on an expensive Kate Spade purse. It seems extravagant and I might feel guilty buying it for myself. But if my husband gives it to me as a gift (paid for from our joint checking account—the exact same money I would have used), it feels great! He doesn't have the same pain of paying because he is excited to give me something I will enjoy, and I didn't physically buy the item for myself, so there is no pain on my side either. Win-win-win.

Your job is to figure out what the buyer needs, what would benefit them the most, and present it to them in a way that will create the least pain so they can enjoy spending the money.

Applying Pain of Paying

Remember: People prefer to pay for luxuries and experiences in full up front; big-ticket consumables can be paid after the fact—and gifts are good for everyone.

Try It Yourself: Is your product something people are excited about or not so much? (Be honest!) Deciding whether you're the carpet or the handwoven rug is important when you determine the best payment structure to reduce pain of paying for your business.

Bonus Opportunity: Find a spot where you can include language like the "small five-dollar fee" to help make it easier for everyone (including tightwads) to feel good about buying from you.

More Pain of Paying

Find pain of paying in this chapter: May I Take Your Order? (25)

There is so much more interesting nuance to pain of paying that couldn't fit into this book. Check out this episode of *The Brainy Business* podcast to learn more about making it easier for people to buy from your business:

- **(Episode 59) Pain of Paying: Why the First Item in a Purchase is the Hardest.** More detail on tightwads and spendthrifts, tips for using tokens and chips as currency, and how to make the pain of paying less of a factor for your business.

CHAPTER 17

Surprise and Delight

HuchtaHvIS 'uy'moH.

In case you don't have your Bing Translator handy, that means "Delight requires a lack of expectation" in Klingon.

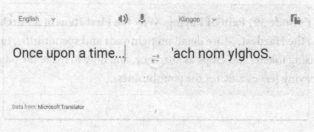

Next time Spock stops by, I'll be ready.

How in the world did Klingon, the language of the fictitious species from Star Trek, get into Bing's translator, and why was it worth the effort? Imagine you work for the team at Microsoft—in a constant battle for another functional update against Google Translate. A traditional view of the business problem would make it seem there is no room for surprise or delight. I mean, why would anyone go to a translator if they didn't *need* to translate something?

Adding Klingon was a lot more complex than it may seem on the surface. Matt Wallaert, author of *Start at the End* and former director of behavioral science for Microsoft, told me, "Because all the words that had ever been said were from movies or TV, you could easily ask something no one had ever said before in the language."[135]

That left a lot of gaps to fill and a language that was intentionally created to break the rules of every language on earth. "You can't say *'hello'* because Klingons don't say that—they just say, *'What do you want?'* " Wallaert said. "With very little parallel text, it is incredibly challenging to build out a machine translation model."

But it created an undeniable opportunity to spark surprise and delight and set Bing apart. *Star Trek: Into Darkness* was being released soon and would have the first characters speaking Klingon from the new series. Matt broke down why this was the perfect opportunity to generate surprise and delight:

1. **A dedicated group for which the novelty is already delightful.** At the time, there were only a very small number of people who spoke "fluent" Klingon—and they were incredibly passionate about it. Inviting them to participate in the creation of the Klingon translator before the new *Star Trek* was a dream come true, and something they couldn't have planned for.

2. **Potential for a perpetual motion machine.** This also meant the translators had a lot of opportunities to share about how cool Bing's translator was and get people talking about it organically. This caused other *Star Trek* fans to be excited and motivated to check it out and see how to say things in Klingon, just because the Klingon speakers were such a vocal fanbase.

3. **Many small opportunities to delight.** At the Hollywood movie premier, the announcement to silence your phones was in Klingon. There were special phones that allowed attendees to snap photos of Klingon phrases around the space and get them instantly translated (including a phrase Matt had shaved into his hair—that's dedication to delight). The best Klingon speaker in the world, who happened to work at Microsoft, was at the Bing booth at the after-party. These are more opportunities to spread the joy and excitement (making people want to add to the perpetual motion machine).

Satisfaction Will Never Be Delight

Many people assume there is a linear relationship between dissatisfaction, satisfaction, and delight, but it doesn't work that way.[136] You can't do more of what is satisfactory to get someone delighted, because "super satisfactory" is still just satisfied.

The customer experience scale instead goes like this:

Outrage ► Dissatisfaction ► Satisfaction ► Delight

If you were to think about the two negatives (dissatisfaction and outrage) and the two positives (satisfaction and delight), the real difference between them is surprise. When you have a surprising positive experience, like a fully functional Klingon translator, it results in delight. An unexpected, surprising negative experience? That is when outrage comes into play.

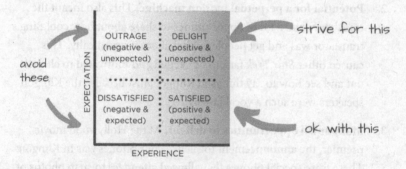

The real relationship between satisfaction, delight, and expectations[137]

Anything that is *expected* lies in the field of satisfaction. If a customer has an expectation, they will either be satisfied or dissatisfied by the level at which that is met. (I expect a translator to have the correct Italian translation—if it doesn't, I will be surprised in a bad way. If it does so perfectly, I will still be merely satisfied, not delighted.)

Ideally, you are living in satisfied territory most of the time, with a few "delights" popping up here and there. Delighting customers takes extra work and can be expensive (though it doesn't have to be). The question becomes, is it worth the investment?

Short answer: yes.

Here is the long answer.

Delight is much more likely to drive loyalty than mere satisfaction, and there is a lot of research that shows loyalty is positively linked to profits and stock market price.[138]

The loyalty curve flattens out once you achieve satisfaction.[139] So, once a customer becomes satisfied, they have achieved whatever level of loyalty they'll have, even as they move from, say, moderately satisfied to satisfied to extremely satisfied.

But once *delight* is introduced? Hold onto your hats, ladies and gentlemen! We are shooting upward on the loyalty score.

Consider buying a car. It is a big deal to the manufacturer to get repeat buyers on such large and infrequent purchases. How much does delight change loyalty for them? In the case of one study for Mercedes-Benz,[140] the likelihood of getting repeat business from customers by group is:

- Dissatisfied: 10 percent

- Satisfied: 29 percent

- Delighted: 86 percent (worth it!)

Don't Get Stuck in the Satisfaction Trap

Satisfied customers are not incredibly loyal. They might appear loyal (say, if you do a lot of special promotions or there is a high cost to switch) but this is different from real loyalty, which is rooted in delight.

Delightful experiences hit the emotional center of the brain (hello feel-good chemicals!), making them much more likely to be remembered and shared (feeding the perpetual motion machine).[141] But remember, this also holds true for outrage, the mirror of delight. This is why negative surprises can be held in a customer's memory bank for what feels like eternity. So be careful when using surprise, and make sure it is associated with positive experiences.

If you're still asking yourself, "Is it worth the effort?" consider this:

- A 5 percent increase in loyalty can increase profit from 25 to 85 percent[142]

- One delighted, loyal customer can have a lifetime value equal to eleven "regular" customers[143]

Think about it. Are those Klingon speakers who participated in the project likely to be loyal to Microsoft and inadvertently refer their friends by talking about it at gatherings and on social media? Absolutely.

Measurement Problem

Customers can't tell you what would delight them because it must be unexpected. And, if you are trying to gauge loyalty using customer satisfaction surveys, it's time for a change. Consider how these two questions would hit your brain if you were taking a survey:

- Were you satisfied with your experience at the bank last week?

- Did the team at the bank delight you during your visit last week?

It is easy to brush off the first question and say, "Yeah, sure" or "I guess so" and give a rating like eight out of ten. But "Did they *delight* you?" That hits your brain differently. It doesn't fit into the standard rule of your subconscious, and makes you think a little harder. "Hmmm…*delighted*, you say? I don't know if I would say I was delighted" (which essentially means, no, they were not).

If someone was delighted in the way we are talking about here—that generates loyalty and referrals—they will know it instantly and you can see it on their face or hear it in their voice. That is because satisfaction is more of a cognitive process—you have an expectation and it was met or not. Delight and its mirror of "outrage" are more emotional. They are the experiences you can't help but share with people—either in a rant or a gush of joy. Much of this is driven by the surprise.

For the Love of Heinz

Heinz could have asked customers all day for ways to be surprising and bring delight, and I doubt many would have suggested *Edchup*.[144] What the heck is Edchup, you ask?

It turns out that Ed Sheeran is a huge fan of Heinz ketchup—he even has a tattoo of the brand on his arm. Heinz has said a third of all its activity on Instagram includes Sheeran, either in tags or in mentions, so Ed's fans know how much he loves it.

One post from Ed resulted in 1.1 million likes and over 10,000 comments—and a TV commercial for limited-edition Edchup bottles with a leafy-haired, spectacled tomato in honor of their 150-year anniversary.

Would any customer have suggested this? Asked for it? Probably not. But it sure got fans excited and wanting to get their own bottle of Edchup. And Ed's affinity for the brand means he was incredibly delighted with being showcased in this way; it seems silly to think of it like this, but Ed truly just loves Heinz ketchup! It is as much of a dream come true for him as it is beneficial for Heinz.

His posts about the experience have included the hashtags #believe #DreamsComeTrue #achieve and #TheDreamThatKeepsOnGiving.

Edchup has all the same elements as Klingon in the Bing Translator: a "small" group of people who are already delighted (Ed and his fans), a bunch of small delights, and endless options to use them to feed the perpetual motion machine.

The good news is, your brand can achieve this without Sheeran's star power.

Courteous Surprise

It's a little depressing that a study found "courtesy" is the number-one thing a business does to surprise and delight its customers (as it should be expected).[145] The good news is, this is pretty darn easy to do and doesn't cost much. Empower your employees to be genuine, kind, and go above and beyond the expectations of their customers; it can make a big difference. Find those moments where you can get outside the expectations and look for ways to delight, like:

- Instead of sending holiday gifts (expected), send something in March or August (unexpected).

- Replace the impersonal birthday email/notecard with a half-birthday surprise card.

- Be present on social media. Have real conversations, leave comments, and respond thoughtfully to emails. Listeners comment often on how much they appreciate this from me.

Only you can see this

Hey Melina

I didn't expect you to react to my story (you just caught me off guard haha)

So thought of dropping a line and letting you know that I am a fan! Love your work. Cheers 😊 🍷

AUG 12, 10:16 AM

Hi! Glad to connect and I do make an effort to always reply to, RT or acknowledge anyone who takes the time to share. I appreciate you!

Resharing content can make someone's day.

Don't let **herding** make you feel you need to send things (and act) like everyone else. That is precisely why you should send something at another time—because no one else is. And wouldn't that be a surprise, and a delight?

Applying Surprise and Delight

Remember: Satisfaction and delight are not the same—unexpected positive experiences generate delight and loyalty.

Try It Yourself: What's your "Edchup" or "Klingon Translator"? Dream big and write out as many amazing ideas for incorporating surprises that will delight your customers as you can. You don't have to do them all, but keeping a Delight Journal will bring joy to your own experience, while helping you come up with fun ways to thrill your customers and colleagues. (And then, of course, pick one to implement and make happen!)

More Surprise and Delight

Find surprise and delight in these chapters: Behavioral Baking (21), A Series of Small Steps (24), The Power of Story (27)

Surprise! There's a dedicated episode for understanding and implementing surprise and delight on *The Brainy Business* podcast:

- **(Episode 60) Surprise and Delight.** More studies, more examples, more pitfalls to avoid, and more ideas for using surprise and delight!

- **(Episode 128) Start at the End.** Interview with Matt Wallaert, where we dig in on more of his projects as interesting as Klingon in the Bing Translator.

CHAPTER 18

Peak-End Rule

Your family is out for dinner at a nice restaurant. The manager comes over during dessert and asks, "How was everything?"

You instinctively say, "Fine" or "Great, thanks!" but if you were really going to stop and give the most thoughtful possible answer—say you were doing a customer experience survey and being paid for your time—how much more effort would you really put in? And does it encompass any more of the truth than the quick response?

Truly answering the question requires considering a whole lot of aspects.[146] Rating each course on taste, temperature, texture, interactions with staff, wait times, ambience, pricing, and more. Each item then has multiple time points to consider—and what frequency is needed to give a thorough answer? Every minute? Second? Millisecond?

All of this doesn't even take into consideration how a conversion chart might work. How many good taste points does it take to make up for a negative ambience point?

Your brain is probably exhausted just thinking about all that work, which is why it uses the peak-end rule.

Instead of trying to create an average of all the possible data points and some seriously complex calculations, you can get a "good enough" answer to the "how was everything" question using this little mental trick.

Essentially, your brain forgets about everything except for the peak point (good or bad), and the end point. The rest sort of fades into the background.

Even if you were being paid to provide your thoughts for a brand, you would do this. Think about your last experience buying something on a website, staying at a hotel, a past vacation, customer service call—it all comes down to the peak and the end.

Ouch!

Kahneman[147] and colleagues famously tested the theory on colonoscopies which they believed to be set up in the worst possible way: the peak and end were both at the most painful point.

So they recommended something unexpected: make the procedure *longer*.

Keep the whole beginning the same, just let the painfulness taper off a bit before completion.

Technically, people are in pain for longer than required, but those in the longer condition said they liked the second procedure better and were more likely to want to do a repeat procedure than those who had the shorter procedure!

Leaving a little time for the peak to taper off and not be the final moment made the entire experience feel better. Why? Because of **duration neglect**; instead of focusing on length of time, we merely rely on those two reference points.

Another Kahneman experiment had people put their hands in extremely cold water for sixty seconds. They didn't like it very much. The second time started the same, but after the first sixty seconds, they kept their hands for an *extra* thirty seconds while the water was gradually warmed two degrees—barely warmer and 50 percent longer in the water, but I'm guessing you know what happened: people liked it better![148]

They neglected the overall duration and preferred *more* time in cold water because it got a little better and separated the peak from the end.

Crazy, but true. Though don't go using this as a blanket answer (never a good idea)—you don't always want to extend the duration. Context matters.

In general, when the peak is negative, don't let it align with the end point.

In the opposite situation (positive peak), ending on the peak is valuable. Think about a concert ending on the crescendo, the finale of a fireworks display, or the most thrilling part of a rollercoaster. When those experiences end on their highest peak, they feel particularly awesome.

Don't Make This Common Mistake

As Jennifer Clinehens explained to me when she was a guest on *The Brainy Business*, the biggest mistake most businesses make when trying to apply the peak-end rule is not knowing the true end point in their experience. She shared a case study about Disney World from her book, *Choice Hacking*, to illustrate the point.

Where other businesses may assume their experience ends when the patrons leave the park, Disney knows the end of their experience is actually in the *memories*. But how can they possibly control that? Decades ago, they worked with Kodak to determine the colors that would look best in photos and painted all the walkways in those vibrant shades. This simple change lifts the true end in the experience, and helps people relive the magic in their memories.

Every business has multiple experience paths to consider. Each individual buying sequence, the search on your website, trying to get videos to play, email sequences, calls to your customer service…each one has its own assortment of evaluation points—with a peak and an end—and those can all add up over time to create an overall experience (memories) with your brand.

Uh-Oh...What Now?

Even with the best planning, negative things happen sometimes. Depending on the severity, it might feel like it is the end of the line, but it doesn't always have to be the end of the *experience*. In many ways, you get the opportunity to determine how long that lasts. Remember duration neglect—people liked having their hand in cold water for longer when it got slightly better in those extra thirty seconds.

Even if you don't have the opportunity to create a positive peak, putting a little effort into ensuring the last moment isn't the worst can have seriously positive benefits on the overall perception of the experience with your brand.

Your customer might be fuming and threatening to leave, but because of **status quo bias**, the effort required to leave will often make them delay (especially if they have a long, positive history with your brand).

Shifting from a myopic view of this single moment and looking at this customer's overall journey lets you find an opportunity to make it slightly better—or even incorporate some **surprise and delight**—to help the overall experience feel better for everyone.

Applying the Peak-End Rule

Remember: Extend bad experiences past the worst point to make it feel better. End good experiences on the highest point when possible.

Try It Yourself: Attempting to tackle every single experience at once could be overwhelming and keep you stuck (why Part IV exists).

My advice is to take an hour. Use the first half (yes, the full thirty minutes) to list all the experiences you *could* work on. Your brain will want to give up after a few minutes, but push through that wall—that's where the gold is. Then, take the next thirty minutes to prioritize—I like to rank each as priority level one, two, or three, and then work to pick the most important process from importance level one to start with.

Now that you know there are only two points that really matter, you can narrow your focus to two spots within that specific experience (instead of looking at the whole thing and being paralyzed with overwhelm).

- How does the most important experience someone could have with you flow right now?

- Where are the peaks and what is the true end?

- Where can you make it better?

- What improvements can you make to level up the experience?

More Peak-End Rule

Find the peak-end rule in these chapters: A Series of Small Steps (24), May I Take Your Order? (25)

Understanding the peak-end rule can relieve a lot of the pressure on creating customer experience journeys. When you aren't focused on every single second, you can put more energy into the ones that matter, and help experiences soar! Use these episodes of *The Brainy Business* podcast to learn more about using it in business:

- **(Episode 97) Peak-End Rule: Why Averages Don't Always Matter.** More experience examples and my tips for overcoming the peak-end rule to provide less biased employee reviews.

- **(Episode 141) The Most Common Customer Experience Mistake Businesses Make, with Jennifer Clinehens.** Learn more about the Disney World example, how to use the peak-end rule in customer experience, the importance of emotion, and so much more.

CHAPTER 19

Habits

You now know your subconscious brain is using rules of thumb to make most of your decisions, but what does that mean for things like shopping? You're still making conscious decisions for most products in the store, right? Let's see:

- You are at the grocery store looking for soup. Once in the aisle, are you looking for red or blue cans? (And without me telling you, did you already know which brands I was talking about just by the colors?)

- What about soda—if you drink "cola," are you looking for (again) red or blue? And, even if you *don't* drink soda, do you know the name of the brand that is blue and the one that is red?

- It's time to upgrade your phone. Do you even consider another brand? Even with infrequent purchases, the choice is based on habit.

- Say you always use Target for back-to-school shopping. I'd be willing to bet, if you saw those concentric red circles in August, you might think instantaneously, "Oh right, I need to add school clothes shopping to the to-do list. Maybe I can get off early on Thursday and..."

Did you see what happened there? It was so subtle. An association in the brain triggered an action (or a desire to take an action). That is essentially all a habit is, a flow through four steps: cue, craving, response, and reward.[149]

Whether it's dopamine, oxytocin, serotonin, or endorphins, our brains are constantly seeking feel-good chemicals. This is why step four in the habit cycle—the **reward**—is so important. Habits form because your brain is trying to find predictable ways to get rewards. Simple enough, right?

And that is where the **cue** comes in. A cue is a signal to the brain that there is a reward around. And that instantly leads to a **craving**. You want the thing not because of the thing, but because of the **reward** the brain will receive. And, as we know, cravings can be hard to ignore. It can quickly become all your conscious brain can focus on (because, remember who is running the show) and, until you **respond** to that craving and do something about it (most often, giving the brain the thing it wants so it can earn its reward), it will keep nagging and nagging at you.

When you give in to the craving and the brain gets the reward, you get a double whammy because you've reinforced the original cue, making it even more powerful next time. (Even if you swear that this is the *last time* you'll give in to the craving.)

Once you see it laid out like this, it is probably painfully obvious, right? A total "smack my head" moment—and that should be a hint that we are getting at the right path. (The subconscious knows what it does. When you say, "You do this" and it says, "Yeah, I do that," it's usually a good sign.)

Attempting to change the *response* is what your conscious brain thinks is needed, but it's wrong. If you want to change a habit or start a new one, the cue and reward phases are where it's at. That's what is driving the behavior.

Buying on Habit

People buy on habit 95 percent of the time.[150] If you didn't know about behavioral economics (like some of your competitors), you would be forced to focus on the 5 percent and sell on logic. This is much more difficult than working with the brain's natural tendencies and enjoying life in the 95 percent.

How do you know if the thing you're doing is a habit?

As leading expert Wendy Wood explained when she was on the podcast, consider if you need to be focused on the task at hand or if your mind is able to wander:

- Pouring your coffee in the morning while mentally responding to an email?

- Scrolling through text messages during the video conference?

- Listening to a podcast while driving?

- Talking on the phone while wandering the aisles at the grocery store?

If you can accomplish the task without actively thinking about it, it's a habit.

Imagine you're marketing Cheerios.

Things are good—lots of people buy Cheerios. Moms consider them a healthy convenient breakfast and you're on the weekly grocery list. The habit is "Almost out of cereal—time to get more Cheerios," not "We need more breakfast options," and they aren't looking for a replacement. When in the cereal aisle, they don't even look at other stuff—it's Cheerios all the way. Those are the people who buy your cereal habitually—and you don't really want to mess with that. It is good to think of cues to trigger "cravings" for Cheerios—like putting boxes near the bananas or the milk. Find other ways to get people who already want Cheerios to associate more things with Cheerios.

But what if your grass-is-greener conscious brain started to notice all the *other* cereals out there? In a world where people can choose Cocoa Puffs, Frosted Flakes, Froot Loops, and Cinnamon Toast Crunch, how can you compete? You need to do something before you get squashed out by these sugar bombs! "We won't let people move away from Cheerios to a completely different brand," you say. "We will stop this before it gets to be too much of an issue!" So you launch Frosted Cheerios, Chocolate Cheerios, Fruity Cheerios, Cinnamon Cheerios, Apple Cinnamon Cheerios—any cereal out there finds its way to a Cheerio flavor. BOOM.

And to not dilute the Cheerios yellow box, all the flavors match the colors of the cereals you are competing with to make it really clear what you are doing.

And you give coupons for all the new flavors to the loyal customers who are buying Cheerios regularly, in case they are also buying another brand of sweet cereal. Seems logical enough, right?

Here's the problem: you have interrupted their habitual sequence.

That person who only considered Cheerios and nothing else has now been introduced to having chocolate (frosted/fruity/cinnamon) cereal in the morning. They might never have tried those other brands before, but now that their horizons have opened—and they liked what they tasted more than plain Cheerios (because, you know, sugar)—they are more likely to try the "originals" your brand is emulating. After all, if Frosted Cheerios are an attempt to be like Frosted Flakes, maybe Frosted Flakes taste even better, right?

You have potentially shot yourself in the foot by turning your habitual buyer into someone who likes to experiment with breakfast cereals. And they might never come back to you.

It's important to note that I am not saying Cheerios should not have come out with these flavors. Instead, this is to illustrate that you should always consider who you are speaking to and what the disruption to the habitual buying cycle could do to your market position. Giving coupons to your habitual buyers could be bad, but giving coupons to those who already buy the frosted and chocolate cereals could be a great strategy to break that habitual buying cycle and give you a try.

Brand leaders don't want to do too much to shake things up. Coca-Cola has a different strategy than Pepsi. Jones Soda needs to use coupons and crazy tactics to try to interject their brand into the mix when that cue/craving starts.

In case you aren't familiar with Jones Soda, they're headquartered in Seattle and have traditional flavors like cola and lemon-lime, but also release unique flavors—like "turkey and gravy" at Thanksgiving (which was so popular it sold out in two hours). Their regular flavor lineup is fun, like Watermelon, Fufu Berry, Blue Bubblegum, and Warheads Extreme Sour Black Cherry (did you feel your cheeks pucker at that one? That's **priming** at work!).

Jones enjoys a large cult following and managed to land exclusive deals at Qwest Field (with bottles featuring Seahawks players available in store) and on Alaska Airlines. They were also the first cane sugar drinks in regional 7-11 stores. While they will never overturn Coke or Pepsi, they have successfully carved out a nice niche for themselves and built a solid brand their fans love.

The habits of your current and potential customers are important to consider when building your strategies. When you are not the market leader, you need to put in some hustle and fight to break through the habitual buying cycle. But, as illustrated in the Cheerios example, market leaders that try to respond in kind could weaken their position.

Consistency Is Key

The world is overflowing with content. If you want people to be excited about yours (so they follow, engage, and stick around), *you need to be consistent to become part of their habits.* And, as a bonus, you can sprinkle in some **surprise and delight** to help get an extra flood of **dopamine** and **anticipation** to keep the habit loop moving.

Nir Eyal gives great tips for this in his bestselling book *Hooked*, and countless companies in Silicon Valley and beyond have implemented the model.[151]

NIR EYAL'S HOOK

The Hooked Model Canvas, from Nir Eyal

Once you start looking for the habit-building implementations, you see them in all sorts of apps:

- Duolingo gives priority privileges for people with over three-hundred-day streaks, and you earn a lingot (their currency) every ten days of a streak.

- Candy Crush and Pokémon Go! give bonuses when you come back multiple days in a row.

- Social media apps are defaulted to give notifications (a **nudge**) to encourage you to check in.

Before you blindly copy others, consider what you want your customers to build a habit around. Pique, an app cofounded by behavioral scientists Sendhil Mullainathan, Michael Norton, and Bec Weeks, was created to help people shake up their routines and do something different each day.[152]

While they are essentially trying to break habits (getting lost in social media and ignoring your significant other, sleepwalking through your day without paying attention to the world around you), they also need you to make one: the Pique habit. Their habit is about getting you to try something new, by coming back to them daily to check out your packs to get help with, for example, calling an old friend or learning the benefits of letting your mind wander.

Habits aren't bad. We need them to survive. Understanding how the brain uses habits, and how you can work with them, is essential for business. One last question to ask is, are you really trying to break a habit, or would you do better by attaching to another one (known as **temptation bundling**)? Wharton professor Katy Milkman led a research project called Holding the Hunger Games Hostage at the Gym, where participants could only have access to their iPods while (you guessed it) at the gym. This uses a tempting habit—listening to that awesome audiobook—and combines it with a habit people would like to build, but may otherwise feel compelled to put off, like exercising.[153]

The participants whose iPods were "held hostage" were 51 percent more likely to visit the gym. And the really amazing thing is what happened after it was over: nearly two-thirds opted to pay to have gym-only access for their devices!

How might your brand creatively use habits to appeal to your current and potential customers?

Applying Habits

Remember: 95 percent of purchases are habitual, and your marketing approach should reflect whether you are the market lead or a competitor. Consistency and predictability are key to creating habits.

Try It Yourself: You should apply habits differently for each segment of your customer base, and for those who are not currently buying from you. I recommend starting with your best customers. When I say "best" customers, this means the people you want more of. If you could only have one type of customer, what would they do?

As you look at their actions, what habits are important that you want to emulate? Where do they behave differently than other customers? Identify how, where, and when those best customers are developing their habits (what are the cues and rewards)? Once you identify these habits, how might you leverage them with other groups (either existing customers who could be nudged up into the "best" category, or brand-new customers)?

More Habits

Find habits in these chapters: Behavioral Baking (21), What Problem Are You Solving? (26)

There is so much amazing content out there on habits, and it is a fascinating field in itself. I mentioned Professor Wendy Wood, whose podcast episode discussing her research and book *Good Habits, Bad Habits* is below, and I also highly recommend *Atomic Habits* by James Clear and *The Power of Habit* by Charles Duhigg. And, for even more on understanding and applying habits in your life and business, check out these episodes of *The Brainy Business* podcast:

- **(Episode 21) Habits: 95 Percent of Decisions are Habitual, Which Side Is Your Business On?** For a deeper dive into habits and how they work.

- **(Episode 22) The Power of Habit.** Because there is so much goodness when it comes to habits, they were given two episodes; this one is all about ways to apply and use habits.

- **(Episode 78) How to Become *Indistractable*, with Nir Eyal.** I mentioned Nir's book, *Hooked*, and his model for using habits in business. He has another book called *Indistractable*, which is all about understanding personal habits and how to be more productive.

- **(Episode 127)** *Good Habits, Bad Habits,* **with Wendy Wood.**
  Widely considered the world's leading expert on habits, Wendy
  talks about her foundational research and what we can all learn
  about habits.

CHAPTER 20

Reciprocity

It's three thirty on a Friday in December. You're wrapping up emails and closing out projects to enjoy having the entire next week off for the holidays. A soft *knock, knock* breaks your focus. Glancing up from the screen, you see Nancy—a friend from human resources—holding a neatly wrapped box. "Sorry to disturb," she says, "but I know you'll be out next week and wanted to make sure you got my gift before you leave this afternoon!" Grinning from ear to ear, she reaches to hand you the bow-clad box.

You have no gift for Nancy and feel the guilt bubbling up inside you.

Unable to control the urge, the words come tumbling out, "You won't believe it—I left your gift at home! I can see it there, right by the door...I'll have to bring it by after the holiday."

Why do you feel compelled to have a gift for Nancy now, when five minutes ago you could've left without a second thought? Why will this moment now haunt your entire holiday?

Reciprocity.

Receiving a gift—even a small one—compels us to give something in return. Not doing so just feels...wrong.

As Sheldon Cooper of *The Big Bang Theory* once said, "Oh, Penny. I know you think you're being generous, but the foundation of gift giving is reciprocity. You haven't given me a gift; you've given me an obligation."[154]

When Penny says he has no need to give her anything in return, Sheldon replies, "Of course I do! I now have to go out and purchase for you a gift of commensurate value and representing the same perceived level of friendship as that represented by the gift you've given me."

And this, in a nutshell, is how the brain processes gift-giving. However, I would say Sheldon got one thing wrong (but don't tell him).

He said that he would have to go out and purchase a gift of "commensurate value and representing the same perceived level of friendship" as whatever Penny got him. In reality, our brains tend to overvalue gifts we receive and compensate in a way *exceeding* that.

Consider the little gift most restaurants give you at the end of your meal. And I do mean, a *very* little gift: a mint or fortune cookie. Do you think this "gift" impacts your tip? Probably not, but that's not what the studies show: giving a single mint increased tips by 3 percent.[155]

Given the cost of the mints, this is a great return on investment for the restaurant and shows that the brain of the consumer feels obligated to pay back for the "gift." So, what happens if you give two mints? You might expect the increase would double—to 6 percent, right?

Nope. It went up almost *five times* to a 14 percent increase!

If we were to say the average cost of a meal out is $20 per person and the average tip is 18 percent in the US, we get to an average tip of $3.60. Those two mints that cost a few cents total would bring the average tip up to $4.10—a full 50-cent increase!

What if a little bit of effort is put in to really showcase that you are giving the *gift* of an extra mint? Would that make any difference? If you heard it anywhere else, you likely would say, "No way!" but because you know how things work here, I am sure you are expecting what comes next.

When the waiter gave one mint with the check and started to walk away…
but then stopped, turned back and said, "You know what, for you nice
people, here's an extra mint," tips went crazy! They increased 23 percent!
(For the record, that would bring our average tip up to $4.43—up 83 cents
from the control group—for two mints and a second of effort).

Clearly, the gifts of kindness and effort go a long way. (But you already
knew that after learning about **surprise and delight**, right?)

And I am sure you are saying, "That doesn't happen to me," or "I wouldn't
be tricked by that," but I'm sure all the people in the study said the same
thing: that a little mint had no impact on the amount they tipped. It
doesn't hit the conscious brain, so it seems inconsequential, but the studies
don't lie. The subconscious feels obligated to reciprocate, and it often
overcompensates. (And, worst-case scenario, the experience is better, so it's
still a win in my book.)

Three Paths to Reciprocity

As with all these rules of the brain, reciprocity presents itself in many ways.
I'll share three of them here: free gift, small ask to get something bigger,
and big ask to get something more realistic.

Tactic One: Free Gift

Businesses constantly give out freebies, and for good reason: they trigger
reciprocity! These are our mints, free trials, gifts with purchase, free
shipping, discovery calls, introductory offers, lead magnets, and opt-ins.

Whatever the gift, whatever the size, giving a little something for free
makes you a little more endearing in the eyes of the recipient. This helps
them know, like, and trust you, while also triggering reciprocity. And
how does someone reciprocate the gift you have given them? Ideally, they
will buy from you instead of a competitor. But there are many small gift

exchanges that occur along the path to continually build trust and the reciprocity bank.

Simple actions like giving you their email address, opening emails, clicking on your content, sharing, and connecting on social media are all gifts from your audience. Continual small gifts and acts of generosity bring about gratitude and help businesses grow engaged fans.

The Brainy Business podcast is the biggest gift of reciprocity from my business. These weekly episodes each take hours of work to produce, and many include a secondary gift of a free worksheet to help solidify the concept for anyone interested (there are now more than fifty freebies available to interested listeners). Each effort and piece of content is another gift in the reciprocity pile.

While people can listen to the podcast for nothing, the freebies are lead magnets that people get by joining my mailing list. This is a free transaction made possible by reciprocity. (I have done two episodes on the power of lead magnets, which you will find details on at the end of the chapter.)

Other free gifts include:

- Sales or discounts (people "give back" by shopping with you and possibly buying more)

- Full satisfaction guarantee

- Free trial periods

- Video series on YouTube

- Q&As with a founder or expert

- Taking the time to engage and "show up" on social media

- Going above and beyond when answering emails

- General kindness and making others' experience easier

Tactic Two: Start Small to Get Bigger

My high school choir was constantly raising money to travel for competitions. Often, this was done via a silent auction, and all the students were tasked to visit local businesses and ask for donations. (Cue exaggerated adolescent sigh.)

Going in cold and saying, "Hi, I'm Melina…want to donate something to our auction?" would almost never go well. "I'll have to ask the manager; we'll call you if we're interested" was a common response that left countless kids waiting for a phone that never rang.

The better tactic is to go to the business with a flyer for the auction. "Would you mind putting this up in your window to support our school?"

This is a much smaller request; one that is easy to say yes to. The trick is to not ask for anything else in that moment. Patience is a reciprocity virtue.

This approach is called the **escalation of commitment**.[156] Accepting the small token means that person has become part of our in-crowd. As they see the flyer each day, they remember us; their brain is starting to think of them as "the type of person who supports this school choir." When I come back in a week and ask for a donation, they are much more likely to provide something for the auction.

Loss Leaders—A Foot in the Door

When choosing a photographer for my headshots, a lot of people wanted me to commit to a large package before doing the shoot. Sure, they had some nice photos, but what if I didn't like *mine*? The fear of wasting thousands on images I might never use made me hesitant. Then I met Jennifer.

Her offer was this: pay a small sitting fee to reserve the day, which included a stylist for my hair and makeup. We would do the full shoot with no other obligation. Once the photos came back, it was my choice which ones (if any) I wanted to buy. She knew the chance of someone hating their images was low, and the hardest part was to get them comfortable and in the studio. I, of course, loved my images and bought several, which I get compliments on all the time.[157]

Getting someone to say yes once (to something small) increases the likelihood that they will say yes again. This strategic "gateway yes" is important. A small yes that is completely unrelated to a future big ask is less likely to pay off, so before you waste an opportunity, take the time to consider the process in advance.

Tactic Three: Go Big to Get Small

While this is essentially the opposite of the last tactic, that does not mean one negates the other. They are two sides of the same reciprocity coin. This one builds on two earlier concepts: **anchoring** and **relativity**.

For this approach, you start with a giant, possibly ridiculous or unreasonable ask to make the thing you *really* want to ask for seem more reasonable and appealing. Consider the following study:[158]

- Group One: Ask only for the main thing.

- Group Two: Ask for a big, extreme thing first and, upon rejection, make the real ask.

- Group Three: Explain both options and ask which they would be more likely to choose.

Here's how the conversation went for Group Two (our "start big" example):

"We're currently recruiting university students to work as voluntary, nonpaid counselors at the County Juvenile Detention Center. The position could require two hours of your time per week for a minimum of two years. You would be working more in the line of a Big Sister/Brother to one of the girls/boys at the detention home. Would you be interested in being considered for one of these positions?"

When they inevitably said, "No" (and everyone rejected this first option), the response was, "We're recruiting university students to chaperone a group of girls/boys from the County Juvenile Detention Center on a trip to the zoo. It would be voluntary, nonpaid, and would require about two hours of one afternoon or evening. Would you be interested in being considered for one of these positions?"

Whenever someone agreed, the experimenter took their name and phone number to be called if needed.

So what were the results?

In Group One (the small-request-only group), 17 percent agreed to participate in the zoo trip (which is pretty surprising in my opinion and shows the power of simply *asking* for things—but that is a topic for another day).

Group Three did a little better; 25 percent of people were willing to participate in the zoo trip.

What about Group Two? When the extreme, two-year example was told to them first? *Half* gave their name to be considered for the program! Wow! And remember, the opportunity is completely unchanged in all three scenarios. It's still a huge ask. Can you imagine approaching a stranger on the street and saying, "Hey, I am putting together a tour of the zoo for a group of girls from the local detention center and need chaperones to give up two hours of their life for no pay. Wanna supervise some rowdy kids?"

I feel like most people would give that a "hard pass" (this also shows the benefit of **framing** and **priming**).

Asking for something even *more* extreme to get buy-in on a difficult request may feel strange, but it works. And, when using this tactic, it is important to have the same person ask both times in quick succession (for the small-to-big scenario, it is less important to have the same person return).

This tactic works well when negotiating. And you may not realize it, but you are negotiating in business constantly: budget requests, staff requests, or pitching to get your idea off the ground.

When entering a negotiation, consider starting with an extreme situation you can back off of to make your real ask seem more reasonable. Though you should be careful your starting point isn't so extreme that it would damage your reputation. It all takes finesse.

And, when it comes to reciprocity in negotiation, I absolutely love the term Kwame Christian, host of the *Negotiate Anything* podcast, uses: compassionate curiosity. Being curious about the other person, and compassionate about their perspective, is a gift you can give them that will make them more likely to want to give back to you (perhaps with a friendlier negotiation process).

A Note About Gifts

The most important rule to remember with any act of reciprocity, is that you need to be doing it without "them buying from you" as your only motivation. People can see through thinly veiled reciprocity easier than you think, and selfish "fake" reciprocity is often worse for you than if you had done nothing.

Ask yourself this: "If they never buy, will I still be happy for them?"

Sharing the amazing world of behavioral economics with as many people as possible is what matters most at *The Brainy Business*. Giving people the gift of a new insight or learning that results in increased sales or better conversations with their customers and coworkers is awesome! Many people share those experiences with me via tags on social media (one of my absolute favorite things). I know there are many out there who get value and never reach out to let me know, and that's okay. I am still just as happy for them and celebrating from afar.

True gifts are not given with the expectation of a return, even when you know they will trigger reciprocity.

Applying Reciprocity

Remember: Giving a gift compels someone to respond in kind—often at a higher value than they received.

Try It Yourself: My favorite way for individuals and brands to use reciprocity is by being overly generous on social media.

We all want engagement on our posts (personal and professional), but how often are *you* going above and beyond to proactively comment on and share the content of others? I once heard someone say that for every hundred people who see a post, ten will "like" it and only one will comment. For that reason, people are more likely to remember those who leave thoughtful comments (you stand out!) and feel compelled to reciprocate.

Make a list of people, brands, or accounts you want to be affiliated with, and go out of your way to share generously on social media. Like and comment on their posts. Share their content on your feed and tag them in it. Tag others in your comments on their feed to introduce new leads to them.

Remember, reciprocity is a long game, so plan to complete at least one of these generous acts of reciprocity a week (ideally one a day) for six months. Then review to see how beneficial it has been.

More Reciprocity

Find reciprocity in these chapters: The Truth About Pricing (22), A Series of Small Steps (24), What Problem Are You Solving? (26), The Power of Story (27)

A dedicated episode on the concept, two on powerful lead magnets, and an interview with Kwame Christian, check out these four episodes of *The Brainy Business* podcast for ways to use reciprocity:

- **(Episode 3) Do Lead Magnets Work and Do You Need One?** The short answer: yes. Tune in for the "why" and how to create or perfect your lead magnet using reciprocity.

- **(Episode 23) Reciprocity: Give a Little, Get a Lot.** All about reciprocity, more detail on the studies included here, and other examples for you to learn from.

- **(Episode 103) How to Revisit and Update Your Lead Magnets, Freebies and Opt-Ins.** The early pandemic was a time when many needed to redo their lead magnets (and business models). This episode presented a framework to create a lead magnet that really resonated during a difficult time (and beyond).

- **(Episode 107) How to Have Difficult Conversations About Race and Inequality, with Kwame Christian.** For the full "compassionate curiosity" framework and more insights from attorney and negotiation expert Kwame Christian.

PART III

HOW TO USE THIS STUFF

CHAPTER 21

Behavioral Baking

Now that you have an understanding of some key concepts in behavioral economics, it is time to start combining them for application. But where to start?

Think about this process as if you were learning to bake. The same basic ingredients—sugar, butter, eggs, and flour—can be combined in different ways to make all sorts of things. First, you need to know what each does before you follow recipes, and, after mastering a few, you can get creative and make some of your own. As you get more advanced, you become comfortable adapting the basic recipes, testing out new ingredients, ratios, and spices as you get more comfortable.

But, no matter how advanced you get, if you don't know whether you want to make cookies, cake, bread, or a pie before you get started, it's going to turn out a dreadful mess at the end.

Just like a master baker, this book has taught you some basic ingredients (concepts) and how they work. The chapters in this section will explain ways those core concepts can be combined to produce all sorts of outcomes.[159] Once you see some of the options and start your own testing and application, you will develop a skill and understanding that will allow you to create your own unique recipes for behavior change that align with your brand.

The Most Common Mistake

"I need a brochure."

Probably not a surprising thing to hear when you work in the marketing department, and ours was no exception. The difference, I've learned, is how I responded to requests like this. Instead of taking that ask at face value and assigning my team to make a brochure for whatever branch was asking for one that day, I would follow up and say, "Tell me more. When do you want to use this item? What are you trying to accomplish?"

Over the years, I learned that "brochure" was a word people would use as a catch-all for marketing support. This was the word they knew, and while it means something incredibly specific to a person in marketing, what the asker really wanted was help. This person had found a gap in their process. Their job was to bring it to my attention—which was done now. *My* job was to understand their problem and help provide a solution.

This was almost never a "brochure," and no one ever lamented not receiving a trifold sheet of paper.

I want to point out that the **framing** of my response was just as important as anything else in the process. If, every time someone came to me and said, "I need a brochure," I said, "No, you don't, you don't know what you want, take this instead," I would have had a lot of unused marketing materials thrown back in my face.

Being curious and asking good questions allowed me to appeal to the subconscious brain, so I could learn about the situation while helping them feel valued and involved in the process. Taking those few extra moments to understand the problem made all the difference.

- The department received something that solved their real problem.

- Someone inside the department was now an advocate for it, increasing chances of success.

- My team wasn't wasting time making something that wouldn't help the staff.

Even when someone asks you explicitly for something, or you are *sure* you know the root of a problem, it can usually benefit from a little more thoughtfulness.

> The biggest mistake most businesses make when trying to apply behavioral economics is at step one. It is too easy to find the right answer to the wrong question. Invest more time in understanding the problem so you are creating the right interventions to nudge behavior properly.

Think back to Part I. Our brains are biased to believe we are right. We also believe that, if someone asks for something explicitly, they did the due diligence to determine it really is the thing they want before asking for it. (Not necessarily true.)

Clients often ask me, "What is the best way to structure our offers?" and similar to the "tell me more" response with the brochures, I say, "That depends. What do you want people to do?"

As you saw in Part II, choices are relative and heavily context dependent. There is no *one best layout*. There is no single, perfect concept of behavioral economics that will work in every situation. There is a great deal of art in this science—that's my favorite part—and it is also the root of the most common mistake I see people make when trying to apply behavioral concepts to their business.

When you consider the problem in a vacuum or assume the problem you see is the only true problem, you will often end up finding the right answer to the wrong question.

The best brochure in the world won't solve a deeper, unrelated issue.

Working with the brain will make it easier to understand and solve problems in your business. I have used it with my own clients to increase conversions, raise prices, nudge product choices, and so much more. But if you don't take the time up front to understand what you are trying to accomplish, you will still be throwing noodles at the wall.

> Properly applied behavioral economics lets you throw darts while everyone else is just throwing noodles.

Change Is Hard

Would you agree with that statement? Most people do. This tenet has been ingrained in us—that people do not like to change and that it is difficult to get them to do anything.

This is true, but not necessarily in the way you think.

Imagine it is now your job to ensure that every person on earth will throw away and properly sort all their trash every single time they have something to dispose of. Are you excited about (or dreading) this prospect? After all, there have been campaigns for decades encouraging people to "reduce, reuse, recycle" and letting them know that if they litter it will hurt the planet, but with the consequences so distant, it is easy to ignore and not change behavior.

How would you feel if I told you that you had to launch and test your program in a movie theater?

In case you've never been to a movie theater (or have simply forgotten what it's like), this is a place where even the most environmentally conscious individuals feel entitled to leave their popcorn containers, empty cups, and any other sticky garbage behind after the movie ends.

Now how do you feel about your task? Does it feel insurmountable? Doomed to fail?

This is not a hypothetical example: allow me to introduce The Littery.[160] This amazing company has incorporated behavioral economics to work with the brain and get people to willingly throw away (and properly sort) their garbage. How?

The answer is in the name: by turning litter into lottery tickets.

Today, when you walk down the street and see a gum wrapper or empty bottle, you think, "Gross. Some people are so inconsiderate!" and continue walking. What if the item on the sidewalk was a lottery ticket instead of a gum wrapper? Would you be more likely to pick it up?

Of course you would! Your brain is programmed to wonder what could be (**optimism bias**) and fear for what might happen if you choose to leave it there and it was a winner (**loss aversion**).[161]

That's why The Littery created smart garbage cans that can tell if you properly sorted and threw away your trash. Do it right, get a lottery ticket. Do it wrong (like putting paper in trash instead of recycling), you get a notification on how to adjust for next time.

You might have guessed that their proof of concept was conducted in four movie theaters over thirty days in Sweden. And there was 100 percent compliance—people were even seen running through the aisles after the movie trying to find additional trash to throw away (they were disappointed to not find any) and women were rifling through their purses for additional tissues or tidbits to toss.

The top prize was five thousand euros, and others won free movie tickets. Can you imagine the opportunity for state- or country-wide lotteries with prizes in the millions?

Now when you walk past that gum wrapper or empty bottle on the street, you might just pick it up and be excited to throw it away.

The lesson? Change doesn't have to be hard.

Changing the natural rules of the subconscious brain that have been developing for generations is hard. Understanding them and working with those habits can make seemingly insurmountable changes—like getting people to throw away and properly sort their garbage—become easy.

I love The Littery's example because it really shines a light on what can be accomplished when a business takes the time to properly understand the problem before jumping in with a solution. You and your business can do that too, and this book will help you on your journey. And while this first step may seem trivial, it is paramount to your success. So, get ready for a lot of quality time with your own brain as you ponder problems!

This part of the book is designed to work through one problem at a time and the prompts will remind you of that along the way. This is also meant to be reference material you can reuse again and again. To help you with that, I've created a free PDF workbook that accompanies this book (with even more goodies and prompts that couldn't fit here), which you can download and print as many copies of as you like as you begin applying behavioral economics to all your business questions, problems, and projects.

Get your free workbook now at thebrainybusiness.com/ApplyIt

Beginning to Apply Behavioral Economics

Lesson: Spend the bulk of your time considering and reframing the problem to identify existing brain concepts you can use to your advantage, making change easier.

Try It Yourself: Choose one vertical, service, or product you will work on as you go through Part III. Write it here: _____

_____

You can, of course, change as you go and (hopefully) use the steps again and again! But writing something down to tell your brain it is important will help it be top of mind as you read.

Concepts: framing (5), herding (11), habits (19), reciprocity (20)

For more on this process, check out this episode of *The Brainy Business* podcast:

- **(Episode 126) The Most Important Step in Applying Behavioral Economics: Understanding the Problem.**

CHAPTER 22

The Truth About Pricing

Pricing strategy is one of the top things I help clients with. Over the years, I've found this is something everyone struggles with, from solopreneurs to global corporations, newbies to established businesses. Everyone gets stuck on pricing.

The worst part about that is the lack of confidence that comes from uncertainty. Just like they say dogs can smell fear,[162] your potential customers and clients can smell a lack of confidence, and it will impact the entire buying experience.

Thankfully, behavioral economics can help you gain confidence in your pricing and increase sales. Let's showcase the truth about pricing with a story.

Scenario One: Imagine you're walking down the street with your best friend. You haven't seen each other in a while, and are having a particularly engaging conversation, catching up on all that's happened over the last few months. Suddenly, a delicious scent wafts into your nose…sugar, butter, chocolate, and a hint of salt…those are delicious cookies baking!

Your nose is now on the hunt to find the source of the delightful smell (remember the **dopamine** release associated with anticipation) and, while you're still half-listening, you've both become distracted. You're essentially cartoon characters now with your nostrils leading you down the street.

When you finally find the store and see a line, you think, "These cookies must be amazing!" and can't help but wander inside. You're handed a sample and told there is a sale today only—buy three, get one free. Before you know it, you and your friend leave the bakery each eating a cookie, with a bag in hand.

Scenario Two: You are walking down the street with the same friend, same engaging conversation, when, out of nowhere, someone shoves a flyer in your face and says, "Today only! Buy four cookies and only pay for three of them! I've got samples!" while shoving a tray in your face.

Ugh.

How rude is this guy? You and your friend, annoyed, decline the samples and begin a one-upping contest of worst sales experiences. By the time you're in front of the bakery and smell the cookies, you're so irritated you grab your phones to write a Yelp review about how awful their tactics are, vowing that you will never buy from them (pitying those fools in line whose standards are lower than your own).

Same bakery. Same cookies. Completely different experience.

And did you notice that all the same things happened (just in reverse)? There are several concepts at play here making up my "It's Not About the Cookie" Framework:

- Priming (the scent of the cookies)

- Herding / Social proof (the line, reviews)

- Loss aversion / Perceived ownership (from the tasting, scent, and scarcity)

- Reciprocity (free sample)

- Framing ("Buy three, get one free" vs. "Buy four cookies and only pay for three of them")

- Scarcity (Today only!)

Priming (the Scent of the Cookies)

The smell of the cookies got your subconscious "buying" brain excited and made you interested in getting something sweet. By the time you found the sign for the bakery, you were practically begging them to sell you a cookie—and then they gave you a sample…and a discount! How nice of them! And it is such a great deal, and it is today only…and your conscious brain is going to quickly logic its way into submitting to the will of your subconscious.

This brings us to the truth about pricing: it's not about price.

Everything that happens *before* the price (context!) matters much more than the price itself. In the first example, you were primed and ready to buy cookies before you knew how much they cost. Similarly, you were primed to *not want* the second cookies, regardless of how cheap they were. They could have been three dollars each in the first example and only fifty cents in the second, but it doesn't matter.

> **The Truth About Pricing**
>
> It isn't about price. Everything that happens before the price (context!) matters much more than the price itself.

Which experience is closer to what your customers are getting from you? Are you accosting them in the middle of the street and shoving a flyer in their face? Or drawing them in with the irresistible scent of gooey chocolate chip cookies?

You might be thinking to yourself, "But Melina! I sell services, I don't have the luxury of a delectable treat to draw people in!" or "My customers find me on the internet! Scent is a non-issue, so none of this applies."

That is your **status quo**-loving brain trying to keep you stuck, and I'm here to say, "No sale" to that argument.

Remember, priming is about much more than scent. Powerful imagery, great verbiage, video, emojis—they can all prime your potential customers to take an action.

Netflix has found through extensive testing that the right image can increase the likelihood someone will select a title (and keep watching it) by as much as 30 percent.[163]

There is power in priming. When it comes to pricing, the wrong prime could make people undervalue what you're selling and close their wallets.

Begging and shoving logic in their face does not work—remember the cookie flyer. You got irritated and shunned the whole establishment in that scenario. This is also why you can't jump right in with the pricing. If you start out with the price and then plan to follow it up with a bunch of reasons why it is a good investment (or why they'll like it or how valuable it is), they will have already tuned out and moved on—just like the poor guy handing out samples on the street.

You need something nearly irresistible to your ideal client. What do they care about? What will draw their subconscious so it is interested enough to get them to actively look for you and engage with you when they find you?

Herding and Social Proof

Once you've piqued their interest with a prime, showing that other people have chosen you is important. In the cookie example, this was the line in the bakery (and your outraged Yelp review). For another experience, it might be the number of followers on social media, a star rating, or testimonials. This step is important to help the potential customer feel like choosing you is smart, so use it often. Look for multiple opportunities to incorporate social proof throughout the buying experience to keep them engaged and validated.

Reciprocity and Loss Aversion

The brain takes ownership quickly. Helping someone see themselves as they will be after they've acquired your product or service is important in triggering loss aversion. The free sample (a gift) accomplishes both in the bakery example. Finding the moment when someone is considering buying and giving them a little taste (a free download, video, great story) makes a huge difference in the buying experience.

Scarcity

Now that they are experiencing a feeling of ownership, built on top of an aversion to loss, incorporating the "today only" special can **nudge** them over the edge. You can also incorporate some **time pressure** with a ticking clock or giving that "twenty other people are looking at this" or "only five left" message. This also brings social proof back into the mix to help reinforce their decision to buy.

Framing

How you present the offer impacts the way they hear it and whether someone is ready to act. The good cookie scenario had a rhyming phrasing ("buy three, get one free") compared to the bad scenario's clunky "buy four cookies and only pay for three of them" statement. Our brains believe that rhymes are more truthful[164] and that those who communicate simply are more knowledgeable. Play around with phrasing and offers to find which frames work best once someone has been properly primed and is ready to buy.

More About Pricing

As mentioned at the top of this chapter, I do a lot of work with pricing. There are several episodes of the podcast with tips for raising prices, talking about how to think about and offer discounts, choosing the right number to end prices with, there is a ten-module Brainy Pricing Course on my website, and I teach a virtual continuing education course on this at Texas A&M University. For the sake of brevity in this book, here are answers to some of the most frequently asked questions I get on pricing:

Does It Matter if My Prices End in a 5, 7, 9, or 0?

As you now know, everything that happens around the price matters more than the price itself. However, I still get this question all the time, so I want to address it before we move on. In general, the final number in your price doesn't make a huge difference. **The main thing you want to decide is** if you are a luxury or gift item (bottle of wine, nice watch), in which case people are more likely to want to pay a whole number price[165]—like ninety dollars. As an example, when a camera was positioned as something to take on vacation (luxury item), people wanted to pay more for it than when it was positioned as something you needed for work or school. Same camera, but **context** matters for determining value.[166]

If you want to be associated with a bargain or deal of any kind, you should be below the whole number. Once you have made the choice to be a bargain, it doesn't really matter if you are eighty-nine dollars, eighty-seven dollars, or eighty-five dollars. That can be to your preference.

Don't Apologize

Priming is a two-way street. Confidence is a prime and lack of it can negatively impact purchase behavior. One of the biggest errors I see people make is apologizing for, or trying to justify, their prices. This never works out well.

The most common place for this is when raising prices. People feel inclined to say something like, "Well, you know, we haven't raised our price in five years and I know it may be an inconvenience, but we've been carrying the burden for a long time and we just can't anymore because…"

Stop. Apologies and justification are for *you*—not the customer.

Prices are your choice as a business, and people are more willing to accept price changes than you might expect. Remember this: you will not be a fit for everyone. Some people can't afford what you're selling, and that's okay. Be confident in what you are selling. When you clearly demonstrate the value they'll receive, there is nothing to apologize for.

A Note About Discounts

Discounts can be an effective selling tool if they are used strategically (say, to trigger **scarcity**). However, what I see too many people and businesses do is use discounts as a crutch when they aren't comfortable with their pricing (see previous section). When the discount is more about helping you feel comfortable saying the number than it is about a special opportunity, it is not serving you well.

My biggest tip is to practice saying the full number enough until you can do it as if you were telling someone the weather or time of day. It isn't your job to determine if they can afford the item or if it is a deal for them. Assume everyone can afford it, and say the number with a smile.

Back in my airline call center job, we were trained to say the price this way no matter what. "That flight from Seattle to Portland will be $2,875.42. Would you like to go ahead and purchase that now?"

(Cue smile-and-wait phase—even though they can't see me.)

The flight before or after it may be $250, but it isn't my job to determine what matters to them. Maybe it is a business trip and their colleague is on the same plane, or they have an important connection to make. You would be surprised how many people say, "Yes, thanks, here is my card number."

Those who say, "Yikes! That's crazy expensive. What are my other options?" have made it clear pricing is a primary concern and we can go from there (and, as you'll see in the next section, this also helps incorporate **anchoring** and **relativity** to make the new price feel even more affordable).

If you're using discounts as a crutch, it's time for a detox. Next time you quote a price, say the number with your call to action and just wait. Do not speak again until they speak. Smile even if the anticipation is killing you on the inside. You'll be shocked at how many people say, "Okay, let's do it!" (and studies have shown people get more value out of things they pay more for, so that's a win too).[167]

Try This Mental Trick

If you're struggling with the idea of raising prices, I've got a simple, game-changing tip.

Imagine you sell water bottles. Yours currently sells for eight dollars and you need to raise the price to twelve dollars. This is a substantial increase, which may feel mentally jarring (i.e., something you feel compelled to apologize for and offer discounts before anyone asks for one).

Take a step back and ask this question: "What if tomorrow we sold this for ten times what we charge now?" This creates a new, **high mental anchor** of eighty dollars. How could you justify or add the value? A special design or a celebrity using it (**social proof**)? Once you can get behind selling it at eighty dollars, selling it for twelve is a breeze.

Applying Pricing

Lesson: Pricing is not about the price—everything else matters much more than the price itself.

Try It Yourself: Gather up the pricing details for the brand, product, or service you identified in the last chapter. What is the experience like *before* they get to the pricing? Begin thinking about the "small steps" approach from **paradox of choice** (we will revisit it again soon) and really think through each moment. Make a few notes on the pricing experience here:

How do (can) you **prime** them to be ready to buy (what is your "scent of the cookies")? _____

_____

Where do (can) you use **social proof** to encourage **herding**? _____

_____

Where do (can) you trigger **loss aversion**? _____

_____

What do (can) you give to trigger **reciprocity**? _____

_____

How are you **framing** the selling language? Does it need to change? _____

_____

Are you using **scarcity**? Where/when could you? _____

_____

Concepts: framing (5), priming (6), anchoring (7), relativity (8), loss aversion (9), scarcity (10), herding (11), social proof (12), time pressure (14), surprise and delight (17), reciprocity (20), status quo bias, anticipation.

For more pricing, check out these episodes of *The Brainy Business* podcast:

- **(Episode 5) The Truth About Pricing.**

- **(Episode 7) What Is Value?**

- **(Episode 66) Ultimate Pricing Confidence.**

- **(Episode 77) How to Raise Your Prices.**

CHAPTER 23

How to Sell More of the Right Stuff

Much as a great lawyer can argue either side of a case, understanding and properly applying behavioral economics can help you sell more of anything. As you know from the chapter on **nudges**, choice is relative. Context and **framing**—the way things are presented—will change what someone sees as the best option.

So when clients come to me with problems like "We were *sure* X would be a big seller, but no one wants it!" or "Even when we offer Y, everyone still wants Z!" or "Our clients don't want to book appointments/work with us that way," I dig a little deeper.

Often, I find the business is doing something to unintentionally steer customers away from the option they really want to sell. With a few small behavioral interventions, the previously unsellable item is now a hot commodity.

Take, for example, a small business client of mine named Mariel. She and her jewelry store, Agave in Bloom, were featured on episode 10 of *The Brainy Business* podcast.

When she came to me, her issue was customers always choosing the cheapest options (which were still of a higher quality than your run-of-the-mill piercing shop) even though she had amazingly beautiful, more expensive options they might have preferred.

In our strategy session, I discovered that, when people called and asked about pricing, Mariel would say something like, "Gold pieces start at seventy dollars and go up from there." She would then wait for them to say, "Okay, thanks" and hang up, hopeful they might come by. (Remember my high school choir example of asking for donations for the silent auction? Similar to that experience, this tactic wasn't converting as well as it could, so we went to work.)

For context, the shop had pieces as high as eight hundred dollars. Her decision to feature the "as low as" option is a common mistake people make. It feels like you need to ease people into it, but this almost always backfires.

Saying earrings "start at seventy dollars" means that that price becomes the **anchor**. And while it is *supposed* to be seventy dollars and *up*, our brains do a little flip and that almost becomes the budget. Now when someone goes in, they are thinking they don't want to spend more than that. Maybe they only bring eighty or a hundred dollars with them. They are in a state where they want to get in and out for less than seventy dollars—and the whole transaction is set up to fail.

The customer might have a bigger budget than that, and maybe they would have been happier with a more expensive piece, but it is harder to get them there when you unintentionally set this low anchor.

So I recommended she change her response to, "The most expensive earrings in the shop are around $800, but we have a wide range of pieces to meet almost any budget. The average person spends around $250, but there are many options that will have you out the door for under $100. When should we expect to see you?"

Now what has happened? That person is coming in prepared to spend more and is excited when they see something at $70—that's a bargain! And maybe they will find something they love at that price, or maybe at

$99 or $150. They are not limited by their brain's silly rule of thumb, and the business has the benefit of more profitable pieces moving through the store. Win-win.

This example uses a high **anchor** of the $800 earrings, which makes everything else look more affordable by comparison (**relativity**).

Duck, Duck, Decoy

The other recommendation I gave Mariel (and one I have provided variations of for clients of all sizes and industries) is to set up a decoy package as the high anchor.

"Decoy" doesn't mean it is bad—instead, it is something above and beyond what most people would want or need. **This is something you would be thrilled if people bought, but the majority won't.** You saw this in the example above (starting with $800 and working down) and it can be used in countless ways.

This is why restaurants will feature very expensive specials or bottles of wine, or a store will put the $5,000 television at the front of the store—they would love it if you bought that item, but it isn't its purpose in life. That is a high anchor, placed there to get your brain ready to consider the items they are showcasing.

Here are the steps to building this out for your business:

1. Pinpoint the item you really want to sell—this is your best offer.

2. Come up with an extravagant version of that, with similar benefits.

3. Consider including a completely different offer to help them feel like they did some due diligence.

In Mariel's case, the "best offer" is someone coming in for piercing and getting an upgraded piece of jewelry (let's say that is a $150-$250 total package). You've seen the $800 pieces as the high anchor, but let's consider another option with more universal appeal.

One common experience among Mariel's clients is moms bringing their daughters in for their first ear piercing. (This is an example of the vertical/product/service she may have chosen to write down at the end of Chapter 21 and would be working on throughout Part III of the book.)

This is a rite of passage most everyone remembers: the **anticipation**—a mix of excitement and fear, possibly a drive to the mall, sitting in the chair and hoping no one you know will walk by and see you cry a little, but wanting to show off at the same time. Maybe Mom took you for ice cream after and you felt very grown-up.

My recommendation: Why not make the piercing experience into a real *experience*?

What if there was a "Princess Package" where Mom could bring her daughter into the shop where a custom sign reads, "Congratulations, Sophie!" with a spread of simple finger foods and sparkling cider, and a special stuffed animal she could hold tight during the process (and keep after)? Plus, a coupon for free ice cream at the parlor across the street, and any pair of earrings from the Princess Collection (which are in the higher price point). Earrings with her favorite color or shape or birthstone are already laid out on a velvet pillow to start the experience.

For a mom wanting a great moment with her daughter, do you think she is sold on the **surprisingly delightful experience** of the Princess Package? I would be! (And, remembering the **peak-end rule**, this helps extend the experience beyond the painful piercing to create a better memory and "true end" point.)

Remember, this is the *decoy* offer.

Like I said, it is something that is fantastic and may appeal to people—and Mariel would be excited to provide it, but not everyone will want it. Let's say the Princess Package is $399. For anyone who doesn't have the budget, now the "regular" piercing experience of $150 (which includes upgraded earrings) sounds like a great deal—and you know it is provided by a shop that really cares about moms and daughters building a fantastic memory.

> Fight the urge to talk about too many things and present all the options available. Remember the **paradox of choice** and how quickly the brain gets overwhelmed. Your job is to make it easy for them to pick their best option. Take the time to think through the experience first and narrow down the choices to make it simple and clear.

Start High

When presenting offers, it feels more natural to your conscious brain to work your way up through the options, but that defeats the purpose of the high anchor. If you say, "Our standard package comes with earrings and is $70. You can also upgrade to bigger earrings for about $150, or we have a Princess Package for $399," it will not have the same impact as, "Congratulations in advance to Sophie on getting her ears pierced! We know what an important experience that is for both of you, so we've put together our Princess Package. There will be a custom banner printed in her favorite color welcoming her to the shop when she arrives, plus a special stuffed animal she can have during the process and take home, sparkling cider, and we'll already have those ruby earrings laid out in case she wants her birthstone. How does that sound?"

It is your job as the person presenting the options—the expert—to make a recommendation and help **nudge** someone to find the best option for them. It does not have to be the least expensive thing available; don't sell yourself short because it feels easier.

You may be thinking to yourself, "That's all great, but how much of a difference can these little changes really make?" **After implementing the advice from our strategy session, the average transaction at Agave in**

Bloom more than doubled. Small changes really can make a big difference when you understand the rules of the brain.

If People Always Choose Your Lowest Option

The way you present information can encourage people to ask for discounts or really focus on hours (making it feel impossible to transition to selling packages). Let's say you're a graphic designer. If you say, "My rates start at twenty-five dollars an hour, and for a project like this I would expect it to be a minimum of five hundred." Five hundred sounds high relative to the twenty-five dollars you started with, and people will likely ask about discounts and how to reduce that investment.

If instead you say, "There is a five-hundred-dollar project minimum. Based on what you've shared about the work, I would expect us to be right in that range. Anything over that will be charged at the hourly rate of twenty-five dollars."

Now twenty-five dollars feels small relative to five hundred, and it makes it feel like you are a safer investment because, even if it is off by a couple hours, it isn't that much to add on twenty-five dollars at a time.

Same numbers, but the way they are shared via **framing**, **relativity,** and **anchoring** make all the difference.

Let's consider a $1,000 monthly retainer option.

If this is the only thing you offer and you say, "I have a retainer for $1,000 a month. Would you like that?" there is no relativity to show value, so it doesn't encourage the brain to move forward. It will instead create uncertainty and make them feel the need to do some due diligence (i.e., search your competitors and potentially never return).

You don't want that. Instead, you want to create your decoy. Here are some options I've recommended for clients:

- Kick off the contract with an in-person day, which adds an extra $6,000 to the total, making it $1,500 a month with a twelve-month contract.

- If you have a standard turnaround time of seventy-two hours on requests, they can get twenty-four or forty-eight hours on turns as a "premium" client.

- Kick off with a rebrand and more pieces each month for a $2,500 retainer.

It doesn't matter what you choose to create here—whatever would appeal to your clients and you would be excited if someone chose it (don't pick the in-person day if you hate the idea of traveling).

Let's say you choose the $2,500 retainer. Now you can say, "I have multiple packages available, the first includes a complete brand evaluation and refresh, with work for everything from Facebook ads to billboards. That is $2,500 per month. Or, if you don't need billboards, bus ads, or rebranding, there is a $1,000 retainer package. Which sounds like the best option for you?"

Notice they are both valid and useful for different groups. If someone needs billboards or a brand refresh, they might pick the bigger package, but the $1,000 package is enough for most people, who will be thankful you created this package for them. It also establishes you as an expert because you know what "most people" need and aren't out to gouge people. You are putting their needs first to create packages that will fit their needs. Nice.

Do note that it is intentional to not ask all the screening options first to weed out whether they need billboards and a rebrand before suggesting the pricing. That would remove the benefit of the high anchor being mentioned first.

Bundles Don't Require Discounts

The last chapter already touched on not using discounts as a crutch, which I want to reiterate here. Lots of people think bundling items mandates providing a discount: it's not true. There are lots of bundles sold on Amazon that are more expensive than buying each item separately, and people are happy to pay more for the convenience.

You can also create your high anchor using a bundle and no discount. (It works, I promise.)

Imagine you have three courses that can be combined (someone can take all three). You might say, "We offer three courses. The first one is $500 and it is on *Topic*; there is also a $600 course on *Other Topic*, and an $800 course on *Another Topic*. Which would you like to start with?"

In that case, you are leading them to the $500 course, because it became the anchor.

Instead, you could say, "We offer three courses, first is the $800 *Another Topic* course. We also have the *Other Topic* course for $600 and the *Topic* course for $500. Which would you like to start with?"

Most people will choose the $600 course (the middle option) in that case.[168]

If instead you say, "We have the Ultimate Package for $1,900, where you get all three courses. Or you can always start with the *Another Topic* course, which is $800. What sounds like the best fit for you?"

In that case, you are making the $800 course the clear best option. Some people might get them all, but a lot will start with that one, the most expensive individual course that most wouldn't have picked when presented in the other two ways. There was no discount on the bundle, but calling attention to the combined price—and leading with it—made a huge difference.

Your conscious brain may be telling you that calling out a combined price is unnecessary. That people can do the math, and it is patronizing to do it this way. It's not true. Remember the **pain of paying**, where saying "*small* five-dollar fee" helped people feel better than those presented with a "five-dollar fee"—it may seem silly, but it works. Make it easy for the lazy brain and you'll see more success.

Unrelated Anchors

If you don't want a package or suite of offerings, you can still benefit from this tactic—remember the Social Security number priming example from the **anchoring** chapter.

Saying, "I have helped lots of people around the world to change their lives and businesses, and I have packages starting at $500" will not have the same impact as saying "I have helped *thousands* of people around the world change their lives and businesses, and I have packages starting at $500."

Throwing in the "thousands of people" makes 500 seem smaller. Let's take this one step further and say, "More than 8,000 people from around the world have changed their lives and businesses working with me, and I have packages starting at just $500."

The large, more specific number is a better anchor even though it is unrelated (and it brings **social proof** to the party too—double benefit).

Priceless: A Fancy Word for Zero

Those great Mastercard commercials of yore made a lot of brands see the value in calling something "priceless." This is a great case of showing why context matters. Those commercials establish a story and draw you in with their **priming, loss aversion, social proof,** and **framing** before playing on the fact that the entire experience is worth it regardless of the cost.

Priceless does not have the same impact when you are presenting packages and you want to take advantage of the **anchoring/relativity** benefit.

Just like "them" was a fancy word for "zero" in the Snickers example, "priceless" does not establish a value in the brain that makes the best offer seem better.

Instead of saying something is priceless, get a testimonial that says, "Working with Melina earned me an extra million dollars in revenue last year—who knows what she can do for you!"

That will do much more than saying "Working with Melina was priceless." It uses an **anchor** and **social proof** to **prime** the brain before listing prices.

You can build your offering to be anything you want it to be. When you understand the value and can communicate it, you will find people to buy what you are selling. Whether it is a product or a service, whether you are at a large corporation or are a solopreneur, if you're selling bleach or designer handbags...the same brain concepts come into play. You just want to pull the right levers in the right order to lead your customer down the best path (instead of inadvertently distracting them with a shiny object that ends up being an old can half-buried in the dirt).

Applying a High Anchor

Lesson: Use your best offer and build in a high anchor decoy to highlight that it's the clear top choice.

Try It Yourself: If you have more than one product/service you've been using, it is time to narrow it down to one best offer. Businesses can have more than one, but not in the same presentation or experience journey. Make a few notes on the pricing experience here:

What is your best offer (the thing you want most people to choose)? _____

How much does it cost (for the customer to buy)? _____

_____

What makes it special (why would someone want it)? _____

_____

What does a bigger, more extreme version of that look like? _____

_____

How does that make the best offer look good? _____

_____

What is its cost? _____

_____

How might you introduce these to a potential customer (starting with the high anchor)? _____

_____

Concepts: framing (5), priming (6), anchoring (7), relativity (8), social proof (12), nudges (13), paradox of choice (14), surprise and delight (17), peak-end rule (18), reciprocity (20), anticipation.

For more, check out these episodes of *The Brainy Business* podcast:

- **(Episode 10) On-Air Strategy Session with Mariel Court.**

- **(Episode 84) How to Stack and Bundle Offers.**

CHAPTER 24

A Series of Small Steps

The average person makes 35,000 decisions each day.[169] If you assume eight hours of sleep a night (which may be pushing it, I know), that means you make 2,187 decisions every hour—36 decisions per minute. That's crazy, right?

It's no wonder your customers, coworkers, and colleagues get distracted from time to time. Our lives are a long stream of micro-choices strung together (most by the subconscious, as you know). If you want to break the **habit** cycle and get someone to change their behavior—try your product, buy from you instead of a competitor, or implement a new process—it takes more than a single moment to break through the clutter.

Over the years, I have seen and advised on a lot of advertisements.

One common trend in advertising (or website pages, Facebook posts, you name it) is to include absolutely everything you can possibly fit on the piece. The common adage is, "Well, if we're paying to send out a direct mail campaign anyway, we might as well include…"

The problem with that approach, as you now know, is that the brain is lazy and gets **overwhelmed** easily. When there is too much going on and no clear direction, your ad will go into the "later" pile to collect dust.

When it comes to advertisements (forms, posts, emails, pages on your website), less is more. I advise my clients to consider this question when creating anything: "If the person seeing this could only do one thing, what would you want them to do?"

The answer to that can't be "buy" after receiving the piece in the mail. There are many steps between "receive postcard" and "buy." Each one should have a clear direction to the next step. While the **peak and end point** are most important when someone is reflecting on their overall experience, one way to ensure people choose the proper buying journey is to look at your interactions as a series of connected moments. As an example, here is a simplified experience journey with a postcard:

1. Notice postcard

2. Read postcard

3. Flip postcard

4. Be interested enough to not throw away

5. Visit website

6. Read home page

7. Click on product page

8. Click on pricing page

9. Place in cart

10. Buy

Each piece and moment have a specific purpose, a small step you want the person to take. The postcard's purpose is to get noticed and be interesting enough to not get thrown away—to not be too verbose (so they continue to read) and to get them to the website.

This can be done with a great image, sure, but what about the other **priming** senses?

Have you ever felt the paper stock before choosing one for your materials? Most people outside of marketing would probably say no, and I'm surprised at how many within the space don't pay it much mind either.

Online ordering systems have gotten us to just trust the recommendation (**herding**), but have you ever thought about what your paper choice is saying about your brand?

Roger Dooley, the forewordist for this book, came on *The Brainy Business* to talk about his book *Friction* in 2019. If I were blindfolded, I could choose his book off the shelf with no problem. Why? Because the paper on the cover is *rough*. It has an obvious texture, priming the reader for friction. It ties in perfectly with the theme of the book and helps him stand out. It is clear he really thought through the experience—which says something about him. It gets your brain to say, "If he thought this much about the paper, imagine what he put into the content!"

When I asked him about it, he said I was in the minority of people who mentioned it to him—but that doesn't mean their subconscious didn't internalize the prime.

When everything in the mailbox has a similar feel, how might yours stand out? Raised sections? Rough texture? Interesting shape?

It may be more expensive per piece, but it can also result in your pieces being more likely to be noticed, read, and engaged with. When you think about each experience point as a small-step opportunity, you can optimize the experience and get more bang for those bucks.

I know it is easy to get caught up in circulation numbers and feel like you need to send to as many people as possible. I would rather send to a thousand of the right people than a million random people who won't engage—even if it costs the same.

Getting attention is critical, and it doesn't have to be as hard as you think.

The Power of a Post-it

Imagine you are an accountant at an insurance company. It's December, and you find an error: all 150 insurance agents have been double-paid on their commissions—a $700,000 mistake.

This is back in the days when you can't fix it electronically. The only way to get the money is to ask each person to write you a check—some as high as $10,000. You're leading a small team on the effort to get the money back. How would you approach this sensitive situation?

Fortunately, you remember a training about the brain and how studies had found that a handwritten Post-it on a cover letter doubled the chances someone would complete and return a survey.[170] You pull out a pad of Post-its and get to work, hoping for the best (but with a skeptical logical brain contemplating plans B, C, and D).

After a couple weeks, you're shocked to find 130 of the 150 agents have sent back checks, and a few weeks after that, all but three have paid in full. How could a Post-it be so powerful?

There are a couple of factors at play here, which I discussed with my friend and Cialdini-certified trainer Brian Ahearn, who was on the team at the insurance company all those years ago.

The first benefit is from drawing the attention of the conscious brain with the colorful Post-it (which, much like the brightly colored versus white **partitions** between cookies, has shown to be much more impactful than the same handwritten message on a cover letter). For something out of the norm like this, it is important to make sure the subconscious brain realizes something is different and worth a second glance (the small decision they need to make in that moment to get to the next, critical step).

The second piece is the power of going the extra mile to write the note by hand. This triggers **reciprocity** and can **nudge** the recipient to take the desired action.

In the years that have followed since these studies first came out, many companies have tried to emulate the result in less time with a laser-printed note that is made to look like it was handwritten. Of course, anyone with reasonable vision can tell in a fraction of a second that it was not—and the result can be worse than no note. You've basically called attention to the fact that you don't care enough to put in effort, so why should they?

Be Genuinely Generous

As you know from the chapters on **surprise and delight**, the **peak-end rule**, and **reciprocity**, there is a lot of value in courtesy. A little extra effort can go a long way. When you have a significant issue like this one, it is worth the time it takes to physically write the notes and place the Post-its. And know that "placing Post-its" could be metaphorical, as there are other ways to draw attention and show you are a real, human person putting in effort. Remembering names and important details (especially before there were CRM databases) has helped countless salespeople stand out.

You can't call attention to everything or it will lose its power, so choose your Post-it moments well. Assume you get four each year max. What will you use them for?

Give the Gift of a Question

One amazing trick Brian and I discussed on the show that can **nudge** more people to respond to your emails, messages on social media, and really any other communication is to end on a question instead of a statement. You will be shocked at how well this works. Here are some common phrases reframed as questions:

Let me know if you have any questions.	What questions do you have?
Hopefully that answers your questions.	Are there any other questions I can answer? Or Did that fully answer your question? Or Did I miss anything?
Let me know some times that work for you.	Here are a few times that could work for a call. Do any of them work for you?
Interesting, I'd love to learn more!	Interesting—what was your favorite part?

Ending on a question compels action and helps make the entire process easier on the person you are trying to communicate with. Yes, this helps you, but it isn't selfish. Watch in amazement as people comment on how easy it is to do business with you—a simple brain trick that is a serious win-win.

The Eyes Have It

Did you know that kid's cereal brands pay slotting fees so they can be placed lower on the shelf in the grocery store?[171] In addition, the character on the front of the box is going to be positioned differently on a cereal for adults (looking forward) and for children (looking down). Eye contact works much like the Post-it Note—it garners attention and makes you feel more loyal and engaged with the brand. How much more? Those who made eye contact with a brand character had a 16 percent boost in brand trust.

Applying Small Steps

Lesson: Everything matters, but that doesn't mean you need to worry about everything all at once. Be curious to find opportunities to stand out and call attention when needed.

Try It Yourself: People who don't break their experiences into small steps (those who don't yet have this book) might begin to feel paralyzed by their own paradox of choice at this point. Yes, everything matters, but that doesn't mean you need to focus on everything constantly. Revisit the notes you took in the earlier chapters that broke your experience into its smallest points.

Did you miss any small steps in your experience? _____

_____

Are there any you can/should add or remove? _____

_____

How might you use a Post-it moment to nudge behavior? _____

_____

Where can you reframe a statement as a question? _____

_____

Bonus Tip: Get curious as you look around at other brands' materials. Asking yourself things like, "What makes *me* click on a link?" or "Why did I stop and look at that particular mailer?" or "Why did I want to delete that email?" or "I wonder if they intentionally put those on that shelf?" are great exercise for your brain. Be curious. Observe. Wonder. You'll start to find the small opportunities where your brand can stand out and break through the clutter when needed.

Concepts: framing (5), priming (6), anchoring (7), relativity (8), herding (11), social proof (12), nudges (13), paradox of choice (14), partitioning

(15), surprise and delight (17), peak-end rule (18), habits (19), reciprocity (20), status quo bias, anticipation.

You saw a lot of great insights from my conversation with Brian Ahearn in this chapter! Listen to the full episode of *The Brainy Business* podcast for even more goodies:

- **(Episode 104) How to Ethically Influence People, with Brian Ahearn.**

CHAPTER 25

May I Take Your Order?

How much impact do you think the design of a menu has on your dining experience? You may assume it isn't much—if it has some reasonable **choice architecture** (sorted by understandable categories instead of alphabetically to reduce the **paradox of choice**), the rest shouldn't matter, right?

You may then think that using behavioral economics to optimize a menu would end with the "truth about pricing" chapter—use some **anchoring** and **relativity** to put the most expensive wine or steak first to help people choose the middle option—but true behavioral economists know there is so much more to it than that.

The Texas A&M Human Behavior Lab has had some stellar success on menu projects. Removing dollar signs, updating layout and descriptions (to include **priming** and **framing** techniques), and other interventions resulted in an increase in profitability for Messina Hof Winery of 18.6 percent.[172] Prices all remained the same—this was all achieved using knowledge of behavioral economics to optimize the menu.

1775 Texas Pit BBQ also came to the lab, seeking a profitability boost. With brisket getting more and more expensive, the margins were much lower on that item than on turkey and sausage, but almost no one chose those two. The lab implemented a few tweaks, including:

- Using easier-to-read font

- Making turkey and sausage the first and second items on the menu (drawing attention)

- Giving **priming** names (from "turkey" to "slow-smoked turkey breast") and descriptions ("smoked slow to keep it juicy and freshly sliced to release all of its flavors")

Simple menu tweaks can make a huge difference—like this 400 percent increase in turkey sales.

The result? Turkey sales went up 30 percent almost immediately, and within six months (even during COVID) they were up four-fold, with a 50 percent increase in sausage sales.[173] And, customers got the benefit of being happier after trying new items they enjoyed. Another win-win!

Similarly, Jez Groom and April Vellacott, coauthors of *Ripple*, told me about a menu optimization project the Cowry Consulting team worked on for a large restaurant group in the UK. The project had a goal of increasing spend by four pence per head.[174]

At first glance, it might seem like the menu was checking all the right boxes: it had some nice illustrations throughout to showcase the brand, white space, and division between sections. But, after testing it using eye-tracking (you'll learn more about this in Chapter 28), the Cowry team identified twenty-one (!) mental barriers creating friction. 98 percent of attention was going right back off the edge of the menu or getting stuck in the white space, as you can see here:

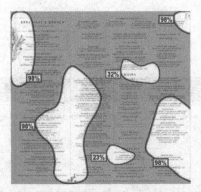

Eye-tracking makes it clear that people were confused when trying to use this menu.

Struggling with a bad menu causes unnecessary anxiety and **time pressure**, so "you just end up picking something you may not be happy with," said Jez, "and that can impact your entire experience with the restaurant—even if you can't articulate that it started with the menu."

Their changes may seem subtle:

- Turning and moving the drawings so they attract the eye to the most important spots

- Adding shaded sections to draw attention toward certain offerings

- Incorporating beautifully drawn cocktails to overcome hesitancy or fear from diners (*What if it's full of umbrellas and would be embarrassing to drink?*)

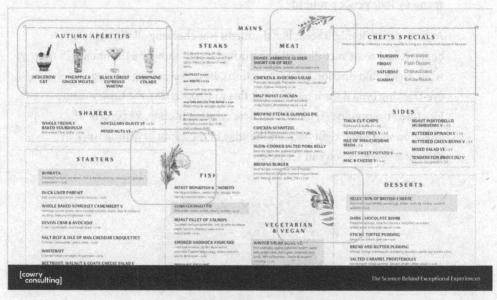

The new menu keeps the eye moving and draws attention to the right spots.

Smart priming images—like the cocktails shown here—are much easier for the brain to process. While it takes three to four hundred milliseconds to comprehend text, an image can be understood in as little as thirteen milliseconds.[175]

Cowry more than tripled the client's goal, increasing the spend per head by thirteen pence.

Yes, You Have a Menu

While the examples here showcased restaurant menus, every business has menus they are presenting to their current and potential customers every day.

Your business constantly presents choices on websites, social media, one-sheets, and more. Imagine the lift your business could see with an 18 percent increase in profitability, or a 400 percent increase on choosing an item that is great for the customer (while also being more profitable for you).

Is your website a highly curated experience, the likes of a behaviorally designed menu? Or are the figurative appetizers, desserts, drinks, entrees, and sides all mixed in together, causing frustration?

Applying Menu Psychology

Lesson: When you provide too much information and don't consider the brain's flow, it can impact the entire experience—even if people can't articulate that it started with the "menu."

Try It Yourself: Consider how the items on your small steps list work together and how shifting them around might make things better. Shake things up by thinking about them like a dining experience:

Which steps need to come first (setting the stage, design)? _____

_____

What is the best first choice (appetizer)? _____

_____

What is the most substantial part (entree)? _____

_____

What sides can enhance the experience? _____

_____

How can you put a cherry on top and make it amazing (dessert)? _____

_____

What is the *peak* and what is the *end*? How can you optimize them? _____

_____

What will make them want to come back again and again? How can you
incorporate reciprocity (mint with the check)? _____

_____

Concepts: framing (5), priming (6), anchoring (7), relativity (8), nudges
(13), paradox of choice (14), pain of paying (16), surprise and delight (17),
peak-end rule (18), reciprocity (20)

For more, check out these episodes of *The Brainy Business* podcast:

- **(Episode 33) Inside the Texas A&M Human Behavior Lab, an
  interview with Marco Palma.**

- **(Episode 131) The BIG Effects of Small Behavior Changes, with
  Jez Groom and April Vellacott.**

CHAPTER 26

What Problem Are You Solving?

"Whenever the goal is to change behavior, the best question is easy to overlook: 'Why aren't people doing it already?' "

—CASS SUNSTEIN, PHD, COAUTHOR OF *NUDGE*[176]

As outlined in Chapter 21, understanding the problem is critical when applying behavioral economics in your business. Now that you have been thinking through the experience—product lines, small steps, pricing, and presentation—it is a good time to revisit the problem before designing a test.

Your brain's **status quo bias** and **herding** instinct may try to convince you that you need to stay the course and stick with the initial problem you outlined. It has latched onto that idea and doesn't want the unpredictability that comes with doing something different now—even if you haven't actually started implementing anything yet. Trust me, it is much easier (and cheaper) to revisit the problem now than it is to realize partway through testing that you are working on the wrong thing.

It is more than okay to revise your problem statement or overarching question throughout this process. In fact, it would be concerning if you *didn't* discover something through these past steps that made you need to go back to the drawing board.

Remember Einstein, dedicating fifty-five minutes of the hour to understanding the problem. You are still very much within your fifty-five minutes. This chapter contains inspiration via a few examples of other organizations that went against the "known truth" the rest of the world believed and reworked their problem statements to achieve amazing results.

Why Don't People Pay Their Bills?

Businesses may assume that people consciously decide to not pay their bills, and so the only way to change their behavior is with strongly worded threats, penalties, and fines. For this reason, penalty approaches (sticks) are common in collections—if you don't pay, you will be punished.

Switzerland has more unpaid bills than nearly every country in Europe, which is problematic for companies and citizens. This led Swisscom, a major telecommunications provider, to call behavioral economist Elizabeth Immer to help increase the number of customers who paid their bills—while increasing satisfaction scores.[177]

Is it possible to get people to pay you *and* have them be happier about it?

For Swisscom, there are a few "known truths" to overcome:

- People in Switzerland don't pay their bills.

- People know they should pay bills and choose not to.

- Threats and punishments are the best way to stop bad behavior.

Elizabeth knew the importance of identifying the right questions before jumping into action. She told me those early days consisted of many sleepless nights spent struggling to uncover the true problem. The result of the tossing and turning was two questions that defined the project:

- Why are customers not paying their bills?

- How can we get customers to do what they should?

"I give the focused research phase credit for much of the program's success," she said. "After the research phase, it was relatively easy to draft a new process." Redesigning the process included looking at things like:

- When are customers contacted? (When do they become **overwhelmed**?)

- On what medium? (**Context** matters)

- What would encourage payment at each point (carrots, sticks, both)? (**Incentives to nudge**)

- What should the emails look like? (**priming, framing**)

- What words (and numbers) should be used? (**framing**)

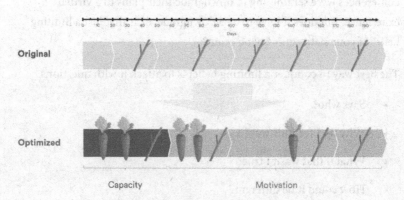

The original process was all sticks, but some well-placed carrots made a huge difference.

One problem was that customers didn't anticipate Swisscom's fines and other penalties. This meant the punishments weren't terribly effective in getting customers to pay sooner (they did upset customers, though!). In many cases, customers were already too far in the hole at the first point of contact to do much about the problem. Swisscom needed them to react before that point of **overwhelm**.

Clearly warning customers they were at risk of a penalty and showing them how to avoid it provided strong motivation for customers to pay sooner. Incorporating some carrots like this (kind **nudges**) into the process also signaled their interest in helping and not harming customers, without the need to introduce any new penalties. The result?

Customers now pay their bills much sooner—and satisfaction scores went up too! In the first two years, Swisscom's dedication to understanding the true problem saved them about $8.8 million.

Virtual Doesn't Mean Worse

When COVID-19 shut down travel, many businesses that relied on conferences were scrambling to downgrade their plans to a virtual experience. But does it have to be a downgrade, or is that just a limiting belief of your status quo-loving brain?

The best way to conquer a limiting belief is to attack it with questions:

- Says who?

- Why do I feel this way?

- What if that wasn't true?

- How could it be different?

- What if the opposite was true?

As other conferences were building out "less than" events, the behavioral scientists at Ogilvy UK took a different approach with Nudgestock. In

2019, the live audience contained about 400 behavioral science enthusiasts; they expected 450 in 2020. The team took a different approach by asking, "How can we dream bigger and create an event we couldn't have done in person?" And, reportedly, they also asked, "How can we create the Live Aid of behavioral science?"[178]

Nudgestock 2020 became fifteen straight hours of free content from world-class speakers, "traveling" across the world in multiple time zones (beginning in India and ending in Hawaii).

It had over 120,000 virtual attendees.

And these were not your disengaged webinar attendees. The day was full of bustling conversations on Twitter, new friends were made, and a thriving Behavioural Science Club has launched on LinkedIn, which quickly grew to over two thousand members. It was an amazing experience to attend, and one that ensured Nudgestock will be a priority on my list for when conferences are back in person. I would *also* pay for their virtual event if they choose to charge in the future.

By dreaming bigger and thinking differently about the problem, Ogilvy was able to create an event that far surpassed anything they would have done in a pre-COVID world. It has built their brand equity on an incalculable scale. And it all started by not accepting that what they had always done was the right or best way.

The world changed, and they didn't let the old norms keep them from creating something awesome.

The Numberless Scale

Can you imagine weighing yourself on a scale with no numbers?

It couldn't possibly work. I mean, if you don't have your numbers to track, how could you know when you improve (or stop yourself from sliding too far in the wrong direction)?

Dan Ariely, author of *Predictably Irrational* (and several other bestsellers), founder and principal at the Center for Advanced Hindsight at Duke University, and one of the best-known behavioral economists in the world, looked at this problem of health a little differently.[179]

As he explained to me during our interview for episode 101 of *The Brainy Business*, the concept of being healthy is so much more than weight, but somehow, we've gotten fixated on the numbers. Transitioning from analog to digital scales allowed for measurement to get even more specific, and giving people their precise weight (to one or two decimal points) seems like it should be helpful—but it's not.

"Everyone's weight fluctuates two to eight pounds per day, and there is a delay of up to two weeks for actions to be reflected in the numbers," said Dan. So there is noise in the form of natural fluctuations, and there is a delay in seeing real results. Together, these phenomena can lead to confusing and sometimes demotivating numbers. "Imagine how frustrating it is to eat well and exercise for three days and gain a pound." (I told him I didn't have to imagine—I'd been there!)

The fear of waiting for the number to show up is difficult as well—how many of us have avoided stepping on the scale for a few days after indulging a bit too much?

As it turns out, the act of stepping on the scale in the morning is much more important than knowing a specific number. This action **primes** your mind for a day of good decisions—which can snowball. If you think about your weight first thing in the morning, you're more likely to remember to plan your day to eat well and exercise. If you step on the scale at night, on the other hand, there's not much you can do other than get a good night's rest.

The "known truth" for Shapa was knowing that one's specific weight is central to being healthy. Asking questions like, "What does it mean to be healthy?" or "Do you need to know your weight to lose weight?"

helped get past that known truth and find their new, brain-friendly problem statement.

"The story of obesity is one of continual small increases in weight," Dan said to me. "A year where nothing bad happens is actually an amazing year medically speaking." Ideally, you would have a year where you maintain your weight most weeks and lose a bit a few times throughout the year.

So Shapa, the numberless scale, became more about those behavioral insights: forming the **habit** of stepping on the scale every day and removing the numbers to be more about overall health.

With no numbers you might be wondering, how do you know if you are on track to reaching your goals? Shapa uses a five-color system. Instead of focusing exclusively on losing weight, it rewards users for weight maintenance ("Congratulations! Nothing bad happened") and avoids alarming them in times of weight gain.

While the typical color-coding approach is to use the stoplight method of red, yellow, and green, Dan and the team at Shapa knew yellow wouldn't be a particularly motivating color. When you are expecting to be in a maintenance state for most days and weeks, yellow isn't much of a celebration (our brain associates it with "caution"). So, when there is no change, your weight is green.

**YELLOW
and RED
could backfire
and demotivate**

In Shapa's color system, green celebrates maintaining, weight loss gets
you teal or blue, and weight gained is shades of grey.

And Shapa is built on *trends*. For the first ten days, you need to step on
your Shapa twice a day every day (forming a **habit**) before getting a color.
During this time, it is learning your normal zone to know what green
means for you (it isn't the same for everyone), so those two to eight pounds
of natural fluctuation aren't counted against you.

Have you ever tried to track your calories and fudged the numbers a little?
Maybe saying you only ate three pieces of candy when you ate seven? Why
are we compelled to do this? Our bodies still take in the calories no matter
what, so the brain is only tricking itself—but it still *feels* better, you know?
Tracking calories helps people lose weight, but only when they are honest.

Shapa solves this problem. You can step on the scale without the fear of
the number. The consumer knows something is tracking their progress. It
keeps tabs, provides a daily color, and lets them celebrate without having to
worry about the complexities.

Making the action simple (step on scale) and removing the fear element
builds an important habit while improving overall health. Four out of five
users step on their Shapa six or more times a week, and after a year of using
Shapa, 75 percent maintain or continue to lose weight.

Understanding that the true problem was more than a number made this possible.

Attacking Your Known Truths

Lesson: Your brain wants to be right and is looking for evidence to confirm its beliefs. We all have "known truths" we take for granted that hold us back. Until you identify and debunk your known truths (as well as those in your business and industry), you will not be able to understand the problem you need to solve.

Try It Yourself: Write three "known truths" that may be limiting your definition of the problem. Attack them with questions.

Known Truth One: _____

Questions to Disprove It: _____

Known Truth Two: _____

Questions to Disprove It: _____

Known Truth Three: _____

Questions to Disprove It: _____

What is our Real Problem? _____

Concepts: framing (5), priming (6), loss aversion (9), herding (11), nudges (13), paradox of choice (14), habits (19), reciprocity (20), status quo bias.

For more, check out these episodes of *The Brainy Business* podcast:

- **(Episode 101) Shapa, The Numberless Scale, with Dan Ariely.**

- **(Episode 118) Behavioural Science Club, with cofounder Louise Ward.**

CHAPTER 27

The Power of Novelty and Story

You are almost ready to begin building out your first test, but there is one more critical consideration before jumping into that last phase. Good news—it's fun. (Literally.)

The human brain loves novelty and little quirks. We enjoy jokes and silly memes, or a play on words that makes us feel smart.

All the small steps in your experience journey are important and deserve thoughtful consideration. That being said, if your first intervention point isn't interesting enough to engage with, your target will never make it to the subsequent points (because they've already scrolled past your ad or deleted the email).

One great way to catch attention and be noticed is by incorporating a little fun.

Cass Sunstein proposes the FEAST framework when developing your nudges (which is an adaptation of the Behavioural Insight Team's EAST model).[180] A great behavioral intervention is: Fun, Easy, Attractive, Social, and Timely.

One of my favorite examples for this framework begins with an extreme commodity: grapes.

Choosing grapes is a pretty straightforward decision, right? Green or red. Seedless or not. You don't have brand names to consider, or farms you prefer to buy from. At least until delightfully sweet Cotton Candy grapes entered the scene.[181] I introduced this sweet treat to *The Brainy Business* audience in Episode 2, "The Top Five Wording Mistakes Businesses Make." Every year fans reach out from around the world, tagging me in pictures when they find Cotton Candy grapes on sale in their area. (Not quite Edchup, but still a fun tradition.)

And that's the point, Cotton Candy grapes are **fun**! They have pink packaging that stands out in the aisle; the cotton candy imagery on the container is **attractive** and makes the benefit **easy** to understand. Because they have limited quantities (scarcity), it has become incredibly **social**. Every year, when they are first spotted in stores, the pictures go up and "cotton candy grape watch" begins (much like the red cups of Starbucks). Lastly, it is **timely**, because people see the container when they are in the store considering which fruit to buy. Do I want the "normal" grapes, or the fun ones? Easy choice.

As you set up ways to apply behavioral economics in your business, keep fun in mind. Yes, this is science, but the brain still loves novelty. If you're bored when creating the intervention, it probably won't be interesting enough to capture the attention of the subconscious.

Building upon the FEAST framework, I want to take it one step further, to become FEASTS. When you look to apply behavioral economics in your business, make it:

- Fun

- Easy

- Attractive

- Social

- Timely, and have it tell a great

- Story

Once Upon a Time...

What makes stories so special?

Dr. Paul Zak, founding director of the Center for Neuroeconomics Studies, has found that the neurochemical **oxytocin** is at the center of storytelling.[182] He and his team discovered that oxytocin signals the brain it is safe to approach someone—that they can be trusted. The release of oxytocin triggers empathy and motivates us to be more cooperative (like the reactions of **reciprocity**).

Zak's team discovered that oxytocin is released in character-driven stories—even on video.

But this only works when you grab the viewer's attention and hold it with a sort of tension. A good story is engaging and pulls you in, whether it's the new blockbuster or a business tip.

This is why the first few moments of a video are so critical. If your YouTube video starts by saying, "Hi there everyone, Melina here again. I'm really excited to talk to you today because…" the audience is already gone. Whereas an intriguing question, powerful image, or unique facial expression could get someone to stop and say, "Hmmm…I wonder what'll happen next."

Going back to our small steps process, each moment in the story (whether it is a video, series of images, or written narrative) has the job of getting the viewer to the next moment—ideally, building up to the moment where they are ready to take the action you've designed in your process. Sometimes the story's only goal is to get them interested enough to subscribe to your channel. Other times, you want them to click to opt in for a lead magnet, share content, or buy.

Well-told stories connect with the memory center of the brain, and people are more likely to remember what they learned in them. Every culture, all the way back to ancient times, has had some form of storytelling.[183] They are part of our nature; your brand should use them whenever possible.

Stories to Save Small Businesses

Imagine it's late 2019. You own a small business and you've snagged an awesome spot on the busiest street in town. There's always foot traffic, so things are good. The city announces a project that will bring a light rail into your area, which is good for you in the long haul…but construction shuts down your street to traffic. They say it will take years to construct.

Your once-bustling spot is now a ghost town. After hours of watchful waiting, only three people and a dog have passed by. The first businesses begin to fail in only two weeks, and this quickly escalates to five failing stores each week. Things look bleak.

This is when Tel-Aviv Municipality brought in Colu, to see if they could help save the small businesses.[184]

Colu understood the problem: decreased foot traffic that was scheduled to last another three years—none of the businesses would survive that. Just like the examples from the last chapter, they built upon a solid question to determine the right actions to take: what will motivate people to buy from these local businesses?

Their solution included some smart **incentives** (for every dollar spent, you receive 30 percent back in special coins within an app that can only be used at those local merchants) and the power of storytelling to engage with users.

For Colu, instead of sending out a simple press release to announce the incentive and encourage people to visit the stores, they included personal stories and imagery.

Discovery | Urban Stories

Tying the ask to a personal story encourages action.

In the first 45 days, over 4,000 visitors did 23,000 transactions at the shops on Jerusalem Boulevard—70 percent had not shopped there before. The $150,000 in incentive money resulted in $700,000 worth of revenue for the small businesses.

And here's the best part: people kept shopping there even when the incentive ended, resulting in an additional 30 percent growth for the businesses. Why? Because customers had become invested in the personal stories of the owners. The stories made it about more than receiving a monetary incentive—they wanted to help and make a difference.

Hope and Empowerment

"You have cancer."

Three words no one is truly prepared to hear, and yet 1.8 million people are diagnosed with cancer each year in the United States.[185]

When you or someone you love is given this diagnosis, where do you go for answers? How many questions keep you up in the middle of the night? Who do you ask? How do you know if the response on Google is accurate or just fake news? And, if you aren't independently wealthy—unable to make it to the best doctors or to fly around for second and third opinions—how can you be your own best advocate?

If you were designing a business that was going to give access to the best, carefully vetted information about cancer—what would it look like?

For many of us, it might be something like WebMD. But for Steve Alperin, cofounder of SurvivorNet, that wasn't the obvious solution.[186] A former ABC News executive, Steve knew the power of story and making challenging topics more accessible.

"Peter Jennings anchored ABC World News Tonight for over twenty years. He was a part of people's lives, so when he was diagnosed with lung cancer, it really shook the world," Steve told me. "After his death, lung cancer awareness shot way up—screenings increased 3.5 percent the next year, which is incredible when you think about it."

Telling people to get screened or to stop smoking doesn't make an impact. Our biased brains think they have time; they like to believe they are immune, that it won't happen to them. Watching a beloved icon lose the battle was the **nudge** many needed to get tested.

Over a decade passed before Steve launched SurvivorNet, which refers to itself as the leading media network for cancer information. It's not a boring, stodgy list of academic articles and it's not about fearmongering.

SurvivorNet is a *media network*. It uses the power of story to help people gain hope and empowerment in a scary time. They provide access to top doctors and actual patients—and it's all produced like a news network. Short, beautiful videos and lots of stories.

It has proven so powerful that SurvivorNet has expanded beyond a website (which gets more than 2.6 million unique visitors a month). SurvivorNetTV is streaming live on Apple TV, Roku TV, Prime Video, and Google Play.

If SurvivorNet can use the power of story to help people learn about and feel empowered through their cancer journey, and Colu can help small businesses thrive, what can your business do?

Applying Novelty and Story

Lesson: Fun and well-told stories can capture the attention of the brain and be your key to changing behavior.

Try It Yourself: It's time for behavioral FEASTS:

How can you make your intervention **fun?** _____

_____

What would make it **easy?** _____

What would be most **attractive?** _____

_____

How can it be **social?** _____

_____

What is most **timely?** _____

_____

Where can you include a great **story?** _____

_____

Concepts: priming (6), loss aversion (9), social proof (12), nudges (13), reciprocity (20), status quo bias, oxytocin.

For more, check out these episodes of *The Brainy Business* podcast:

- **(Episode 54) Biases Toward Novelty and Stories.**

- **(Episode 113) How to Use Behavioral Economics to Create Thriving Cities, with Colu.**

CHAPTER 28

Test, Test, Test

Imagine you conducted a global survey of people who have not yet done business with you and asked, "What one thing would you like to know more of before signing up?" and 46 percent of them all said the same thing. It is something you can do easily, and your staff and production team have been advocating to add this same thing for years because they too see it as a barrier to entry.

What would you do?

Do you say, "Great! Let's build it." Or do you stop and run a test (or ten)?

In many businesses, the mindset is likely that the survey *was* the test. You did some due diligence, asked the question, and nearly *half* of people identified this thing, so there must be at least *some* truth in it. You might be inclined to push forward and implement it as quickly as possible.

Fortunately for Netflix, they did *not* take this seemingly logical approach.[187]

The top barrier to entry was the inability to see the content catalog before signing up for the free trial. Totally logical—but they still ran some tests.

The team set up a series of A/B tests to determine which new version would be best. They fully expected all the new versions would outperform the existing version—after all, nearly half of people said it was the one thing that was preventing them from signing up. The test was expected to determine which new design increased conversions the most.

Round one is Control (no content visible) versus Test Version One. *Control wins.*

Control moves on to compete against Test Version Two. Control wins again. And again. And *again.*

The version without content converted better every single time.

What in the world has happened here? According to Navin Iyengar at a presentation at UX London, they could tell that people were getting **overwhelmed by choices** and options. They began searching for specific titles and couldn't experience the magic of using Netflix.

Users' conscious brains thought they would prefer something, but too many choices overwhelmed them and resulted in a decrease in free trial signups. And while it wasn't explicitly stated in any of the case study material, I would venture to say that the **dopamine** release from the **anticipation** of finding out what was available would also motivate people to get over the "sign up for a trial period" hump. When there is no anticipation or curiosity, why click the button?

For Netflix, which signs up millions of new subscribers every quarter,[188] going straight to market with their survey findings could have had a catastrophic effect on their earnings. Thankfully, they have a stellar behavioral team and a culture built on testing.

This reiterates what you learned at the beginning of Part III: just because people believe they want something, that doesn't mean they do. Just because you're *sure* something will work (even implementing some of the concepts in this book), that doesn't mean they will be a magic bullet.

And, as I have explained to my clients and countless audiences, if you don't test, there is no way to know how much better your solution did than something else you might have tried. Or how much better things could have been if you had done something else.

Dectech, a consultancy in the UK running experiments for clients through their Behaviourlab, a randomized controlled trial platform, has countless studies that showcase the importance of testing.[189]

One of them was around "white lie" fraud opportunities (like listing another driver on forms for a lower premium or saying that stolen laptop was worth a hundred more than reality). These little actions add up and were estimated to cost one billion pounds per year (which causes everyone's premiums to go up, creating a vicious cycle). Opportunistic fraud is not typically premeditated but is an on-the-spot decision by otherwise good people.

So Dectech set up a test of five concepts (norming/**social proof**, self-consistency, **priming**, **framing**, and **reciprocity**) over eighteen scenarios to see what worked best.

Nearly every intervention had a positive impact and reduced dishonest responses in a simulated claim process, but the test was needed to know which ones worked *best*. These ranged from an "honesty pledge" which had a 5 percent bump, to the statistics showing how honest others were, which reduced lying by 74 percent. If they had just gone with the honesty pledge when it had a 5 percent bump, they would have lost out on hundreds of millions.

The only way to know which concepts work in your context (and to what degree) is to test.

Sometimes, the crazy thing that gets thrown in "just to see what happens" will be the intervention that works best. Steve Wendel, head of behavioral science at Morningstar and author of *Designing for Behavior Change*, told me about a series of tests they ran to see which scenario would get people to change their behavior to avoid foreign ATM fees.[190] All the obvious stuff didn't do too much, but an image of an ATM monster eating money did the trick. (I bet it was Fun, Easy, Attractive, Social, Timely, and telling a Story about what happens to your money!)

And while it would be nice if we all had giant budgets and over 180 million subscribers to use for A/B tests, you don't need to be Netflix to benefit from constant testing.

Testing on Your Own

As you move forward into the world of applying behavioral economics in your business, I recommend you start with these three things in mind when setting up your experiments: keep it small, be thoughtful, and test often.

Keep It Small

It's not a fluke that the Netflix example was a series of simple A/B tests; they use the same simple framework on all sorts of things. They used A/B testing to discover that the right image can result in as much as a 30 percent increase in likelihood that someone will watch a title.[191] Google used A/B testing to find the perfect shade of blue for their links, which they have said results in an extra $200 million in ad revenue each year.[192]

When you test too many things at once (turn the text into a button, change the color, change the words, move the location, and add an image), you can't pinpoint what made the difference and then use that information to learn why. As my colleague Dr. Marco Palma says, "If you have a headache and take six different things together, when the headache goes away, you can't know which one did the trick and what to use next time. It's better and less costly to try one thing and wait a while to see if it works before moving on to the next thing."

Keeping your experiments small will help you learn and implement the findings so you can replicate them.

BE Thoughtful

Every email and episode of *The Brainy Business* podcast closes with this phrase, and for good reason. What does it mean to be thoughtful?

For one thing, being thoughtful is about overcoming those known truths and limiting beliefs. Asking lots of questions to find opportunities and uncharted waters others miss.

It also means taking the time to plan before you jump into a test (using the framework in this book as a guide). Even if you are only testing small items, they could consume a huge amount of time if you aren't careful. Doing multiple versions of every email, post, website page, and mailer could quickly become a full-time job for a couple of people in design and analysis.

Instead of testing everything, test the *right* things.

Before you start building a test, know what problem you are trying to solve—and why solving it matters. What are you trying to achieve, and why does it matter for your business?

This is useful for a couple of reasons.

First, it can narrow your focus, so you aren't scattered. That means you can be more efficient with your time and dedicate enough resources to implement what you learn and continually get better. Anything can be worth testing, but everything can be a waste of time if you don't have a clear focus and goal.

Second, it helps communicate the "why" behind studies and your organization in general.

- **If your company is about driving value**, then focus your tests to reflect that. What allows you to spend less on advertising so you can give bigger discounts? How can you showcase products most effectively?

- **If your company is focused on converting** existing leads into customers, increasing open rates and clicks is more important.

- **If you have an application process**, do you know where people get stuck? Why? What would get them all the way through? Does a certain type of customer get stuck, or is it everyone? And are the *right* people the ones getting stuck, effectively reducing the workload for processing staff?

Make sure the juice is worth the squeeze so you aren't putting a huge amount of time and effort into something that will never pay for itself.

Being thoughtful up front allows you to build tests, projects, and products with intention so you can continually learn and improve.

A Note on Generalizability

The results of one test will not necessarily hold true in every situation or for every business.

Remember, context matters. A red "buy now" button on Facebook will have more impact than on Target's website because of the contrast.[193]

Being thoughtful in the building phase will provide some context for how you might try to extend the findings reasonably in another context.

And word to the wise: you can't dig deeper on information you didn't set up for in advance. If you know you'll want to dig into demographics and other details, build that into your data pull up front. Take the time to consider what you may want to know and how you will use the insights before building out your tests.

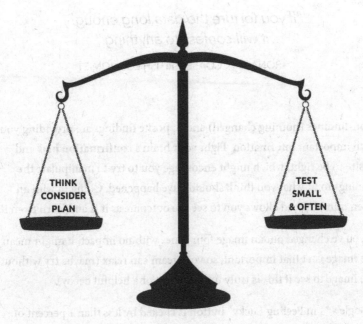

THINK
CONSIDER
PLAN

TEST
SMALL
& OFTEN

There's a balance between keeping it small and thinking through everything you could possibly do.

Test Early and Often

Small internal tests let you act quickly. The more you test, the more you learn, and the easier it gets. Each test is an opportunity to learn, question, and set up another test.

As you begin working on your own experiments, be prepared for outcomes you didn't expect or consider in advance—that happens to us all! As you've seen in some of the examples here, often the unexpected things are the most interesting ones to dig into. I've learned so much more by saying, "I wonder why that happened?" than continually trying to prove the original hypotheses.

*"If you torture the data long enough,
it will confess to anything."*

–RONALD H. COASE, BRITISH ECONOMIST

Non-findings (nothing changed) and opposite findings are providing you with important information. Fight your brain's **confirmation bias** and desire to be right, which might encourage you to try to manipulate the findings to fit what you think should have happened. Going in with an open mind instead allows you to see the outcome as it is and learn from it.

If you've changed out an image four times with no impact, it might mean the image isn't that important, so your team can relax (maybe try without the image to see if this is truly unimportant or a helpful decoy).

Google's "I'm Feeling Lucky" button is clicked by less than 1 percent of visitors—and it costs them a reported $100 million in lost ad revenue every year.[194] Why keep it? After continual testing for twenty years, it has been found to encourage more people to see their search results the traditional way when it's there (even though most don't click it). Gaining the ad revenue from removing the button would actually cost them more from abandoned searches—something they only know because they continue to test.

When your own data surprises you, be thankful for the opportunity to ask why, and dig deeper with an open mind.

For High-Profile Projects

Testing internally is great, and there is a lot you can do and achieve on your own applying what you have learned in this book. But sometimes there are those projects—you know the ones—where there is a lot riding on the outcome. For those projects, I recommend bringing in a research partner.

As the intention of this book is to give you the tools you need to apply behavioral economics yourself, I intentionally didn't talk too much about the science the field is built upon.

For decades, marketing and brand professionals from around the world have struggled to convey the value of their discipline. Perhaps you've encountered someone who has said (or you yourself have believed) that marketing is a "soft" area, based on guesswork and intuition instead of hard numbers and facts.

Behavioral economics gives marketers the tools to quantify and explain their value. This is why I feel it is the future of marketing, branding, and overall business strategy. I predict that, over the next decade, it will become foundational in business programs around the world.

What does the science show us? Without getting too technical, a lot! At the Texas A&M Human Behavior Laboratory,[195] in partnership with iMotions,[196] we can simultaneously track six hundred data points per second, including:

- The **eyes** scan the environment two to three times every second. What are they looking at in those micro-movements? Is there something their eyes repeatedly come back to?

- When they looked at that item, what happened to their **facial expression**? For example, if their brow is furrowing, the increased attention could mean they are confused.

- How long did it take them to **make a decision**? Millisecond delays can say a lot.

- Were they excited by the display? Or surprised? We can watch their **heart rate** in real time along with tracking their **skin** to see if there was a tiny amount of sweat produced, indicating engagement.

- Did they lean in or move away from the screen as this was happening? A change in **distance from the screen** can be very telling. Did their **pupils dilate** at all?

- And what was simultaneously happening with all the **neural signals in the brain** amidst all these other data points? An EEG helps tie the whole story together.

In essence, the science unlocks the mystery of the road the brain is taking the journey along, instead of only knowing the destination. And, once we have seen the journey enough times, we can more accurately predict when others are on the same journey (and the destination they are headed toward).

We can predict with up to 84 percent accuracy whether or not someone will buy just by watching these data points—without ever having to ask them the question.[197]

Testing The Brainy Business Website

Redesigning my website in preparation for *What Your Customer Wants and Can't Tell You* was a great opportunity to work directly with iMotions just like I might on behalf of a client. We looked at the old website to see what was working and what could be improved and tested it against a mock-up of what the new site could look like. Many concepts, including **framing, priming, reciprocity,** and **social proof,** were included in the initial test.

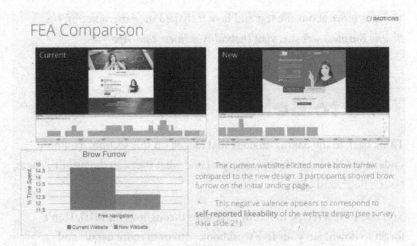

Furrowed brows show where and when people were confused—we knew
exactly what they were looking at and what to fix for the new site.

We found that "Let's Chat" as a call to action didn't work nearly as well as
"Start Your Own Project." This discovery led to more questions: is that due
to the proximity of a compelling image or because of the words themselves?
Subsequent testing will tell, and by the time you are reading this book we
will have rolled out the new site so you can see for yourself!

Eye-tracking software from iMotions shows where people are looking and where the gaps are.

To learn more about the test and how it shaped the experience of *The Brainy Business* website, visit *thebrainybusiness.com/ApplyIt*.

Time to Bake

Think back to the baking analogy that kicked off this section. You now understand the ingredients (concepts) and what they can do, just like sugar, butter, flour, and eggs.

You also have a recipe to follow (the steps throughout Part III). Don't forget to download your free workbook with even more details and prompts that you can work through again and again. Get yours at *thebrainybusiness.com/ApplyIt*.

As you practice and begin to perfect those processes, you will gain the confidence to mix in some different spices and create your own recipes. There may be some strange reactions from time to time, but that doesn't mean you should give up.

And, while you're comfortable making all the birthday cakes, when the weddings roll around, you bring in a professional. (I'm here to help!)

You're almost ready to begin applying behavioral economics in your business. (Yay!) The final section of this book is about some common brain tricks that would otherwise keep you stuck in the status quo. Make sure you don't skip that last part; it will put you on the path to ultimate success!

Applying Testing

Lesson: You never know until you test. Bring in a professional partner for critical projects, and when testing on your own, remember to keep it small, be thoughtful, and test often.

Try It Yourself: This chapter contained a lot of steps to conduct your own tests, so I won't repeat them here. Instead, here are three quick things to consider before you begin:

What is the goal of your first test? _____

_____

Will you do it on your own or use a research partner? _____

_____

Will you share the plan/results with Melina on social media? I hope so!

_____

(find me as **@thebrainybiz** everywhere)

Concepts: framing (5), priming (6), social proof (12), paradox of choice (14), reciprocity (20), status quo bias, anticipation.

For more behavioral economics, check out all the episodes of *The Brainy Business* podcast at *thebrainybusiness.com/podcast.*

PART IV

DON'T GET STUCK

CHAPTER 29

The Forces Against You

Have you ever been to a conference, watched a great webinar, or read a book and thought, "I'm so excited to implement this when I get into the office on Monday!" Then, the routine sneaks up on you and, before you know it, all those great ideas are collecting dust on a proverbial shelf?

I don't want that for you anymore.

You deserve to act on all you've unlocked from this book. Beating the subconscious at its own game is a lot easier when you understand the tools it is using to keep you stuck—that's what this final part is about.

Why does this happen to us all? One big reason is the brain's bias for the status quo, which you learned about in Part I. Think about it: the subconscious is doing most of the work using rules of thumb. Your reality is built based on the brain's ability to predict what will happen next. When it can't predict, it means more work for the conscious brain, and the subconscious doesn't like that.

It has lots of little tricks—roadblocks—to put in your way and keep you doing things the way you always have, where it feels safe.

But you know applying behavioral economics in your life and business is important.

- It will help your endeavors be more successful.

- It can nudge people to respond to your emails or click on your ads.

- It can boost loyalty scores and help customers be happier in all their interactions with you.

Your brain keeps its biases hidden, and everything feels scarier when it is dark and unknown. So, let's get a flashlight and shed some light on these mental-block monsters.

Time Discounting

Ever decided on Saturday night that you were going to buckle down and start a diet and exercise plan "on Monday"? Maybe you spent all Sunday planning and were psyched when you set your alarm that night, but felt like a completely different (and unmotivated) person when the alarm went off?

That's time discounting at work (or as I like to call it, the "I'll start Monday effect").

Studies have shown that the brain sees our future self (whom you are committing to get up at five o'clock to run) as a completely different person.[198] It's easy to commit *Future You*, but when Real You faces the harsh reality of the alarm, it is easier to hit snooze (making it Future You's problem again).

If you want to overcome time discounting to start applying behavioral economics in your business, the best tip is to find something you can do right now. Start today, with a thoughtful question or brushing your teeth with the other hand (studies show this can make your whole day more creative).[199] When you feel like you want to put something off until tomorrow, ask why.

And follow that up with, "What can I do right now to prove to my brain this is important?" (And go do it.)

[Learn more about time discounting in episode 51 of *The Brainy Business* podcast.]

Optimism Bias and Planning Fallacy

Have you ever said (or thought) any of the following?

- "I know I only got two things done on my to-do list today, but tomorrow I'll get twelve more because I got those out of the way!"

- "Two minutes until that next meeting starts? I can knock out these emails really quick…"

- "It usually takes five hours to complete that project, but I bet I can do it in three this time because…"

These statements (of which I am a huge victim myself) are caused by planning fallacy and other forms of optimism bias. The brain wants to think that it will be better tomorrow than it was today: faster, more creative, and more efficient all at once.

We tend to ignore the external inevitabilities that will get in our way (phone calls, email emergencies, unplanned meetings, lunch breaks), but those little things add up. Not planning for them is planning to come in late, over budget, and full of stress.

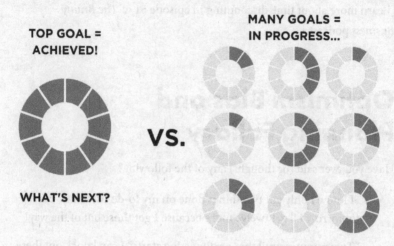

TOP GOAL = ACHIEVED!

MANY GOALS = IN PROGRESS...

VS.

WHAT'S NEXT?

It's far better to finish one big thing at a time than to tread water on ten things at once.

Because the brain feels superhuman, it likes to trick you into thinking that planning to get less done is a failure. Can you imagine starting your day tomorrow and only having one item on your "must do" list?

Yes, one.

Does the sheer notion make you uncomfortable? Why?

Why do we feel better about having ten things we know will never all get done (and then feeling awful when they don't) than about starting with one and feeling glorious when two are completed?

The way to flip your brain on this and turn the tendency into a positive is to reframe with a **new anchor**. When you have ten items on your to-do list and only complete three, you inevitably feel like a failure. The next day is set up to fail, as you have seven of today's tasks plus all of tomorrow's items. It's hard to sleep, as the stress and anxiety keeps your brain reeling.

If instead you only had one thing that you absolutely must do tomorrow—you can't "clock out" or let your head hit the pillow until that single thing is done—it is a lot harder to ignore. And, when you finish it and have enough time left over to complete two *more* things? You feel amazing!

You're a superhero! You sleep better and wake up refreshed, ready to tackle tomorrow's one thing.

How do you know which "one thing" is important and how to prioritize? It starts with narrowing your goals to only have three (yes, three *total* across life and business). I help a lot of clients with mindset work like this, and there is a free mini course available to you called "Master Your Mindset" at *thebrainybusiness.com/MYM* which will walk you through the process. It includes videos from me and worksheets to help you narrow your goals and begin on the path to accomplishing anything one small step at a time.

[Learn more about Optimism Bias and Planning Fallacy in episodes 34 and 114 of *The Brainy Business* podcast.]

Bikeshedding

- Yeah, I know I need a new website, but I can't write copy until I go through all 85,000 templates

- If I want to grow my social media following, I need to research all the influencers before starting (cue Instagram rabbit hole)

- I want to start applying behavioral economics in my business, but I should read ten more books first

These instincts—to continue to productively procrastinate on something that seems important but isn't—are known as bikeshedding.[200] The term gets its name from a group that was assigned to design a nuclear plant but spent an inordinate amount of time worrying about how to design the bike shed. This trivial detail had less severe consequences if it went wrong, and so it felt safer to focus on.

Looking at it from a distance, this is clearly ridiculous. But as those bullet points show, we all do it constantly. The thing your brain is telling you is critical in this moment—that you *must* do before you get to the big scary thing that is your actual goal? It's very possibly a distraction.

In his bestselling book *Indistractable*, Nir Eyal shared an amazing insight that changed my life (and countless others I'm sure). The opposite of distraction is *traction*. You cannot know if something is a distraction until you know what it is distracting you from.[201]

Social media is critical to my business success. I need to spend time there, but when I should be working on something else (like writing a podcast episode, magazine article, or this book), it is a distraction—my bike shed.

Once you have narrowed your goals and have the one thing you need to complete today to reach that amazing goal, your brain will still put safer, seemingly important (and urgent) tasks in your way to keep you stuck.

Should you do this thing right now? Check the URGENT / IMPORTANT scale:

URGENT not important Probably not worth doing	URGENT IMPORTANT Do these things first
not urgent not important Don't do these things!	not urgent IMPORTANT Schedule these out

Use the "urgent" versus "important" scale to help determine if a task is your bike shed.

If a task you identified as your one thing still isn't getting done, the other items you are doing through the day are likely bikeshedding. When your brain wants to do them (often out of habit), ask yourself, "Do I really want and need to do this right now? Or am I just bikeshedding?"

You can see how these brain tricks can combine to keep you stuck. At this point, time discounting and optimism bias will tell you that you will do better tomorrow (or in an hour). Don't fall for it!

Do something right now before you can move to the bikeshedding task. Take one small step and set a timer to force action. If my subconscious is demanding I go get a snack or scroll Instagram or check my email when I'm supposed to be writing, I'll set the timer for fifteen minutes. I need to write for fifteen minutes and if I still want to do that thing after that time, I'm free to do so (but with a timer set so it doesn't last the rest of the day).

[Learn more about bikeshedding in episode 99 of *The Brainy Business* podcast.]

You'll be amazed at how much more you accomplish now that you understand these brain tricks and can avoid them. It will take practice (you're teaching your conscious brain to overwrite rules your subconscious loves) but soon they will become a **habit** and it will be much easier, I promise!

CHAPTER 30

Who Am I To...?

Another way our brains keep us stuck is by using our own insecurities against us. Say you're considering starting a podcast of your own. Your bikeshedding tendencies may come about when your brain says:

- "Who would listen to *you*?" (imposter syndrome)

- "Until your ideas/cover art/website are as good as [name], you can't launch" (perfectionism)

- "What if no one listens and they laugh at me?" (fear of failure)

- "What if it's a huge success and I don't have time to do my job and need to hire someone—I can't afford that!" (fear of success)

To think about overcoming brain objections like these, I want you to imagine a giant weed in your garden. It may have been there for weeks, constantly growing and stealing nutrients from its neighbors even when it's out of sight.

How might you remove it if you weren't educated on plant anatomy?

- Cut the flower off the top?

- Pull at the leaves?

- Run it over with the lawnmower?

While these might work temporarily (or at least look better at a distance), until you get the right tool and remove a weed at the root, it will keep coming back.

It's the same with mindset work.

Until now, you didn't have the right tools or understand the makeup of the "weed"—your biggest mindset block. You notice it, it bothers you, maybe you poked at it a little or pulled at its metaphorical leaves, but you never really got to the root. And you definitely didn't have the right tool to remove the whole system properly. Maybe you got close, digging around in the dirt, but that just seemed to cause more problems, so you forgot the whole thing.

And, once you pull the biggest weed, it seems like three smaller ones pop up. And there's another over there…the more proactive maintenance you do on weeds in the yard, the easier it is to pull the small ones that will inevitably grow.

It's the same with mental blocks in your brain. They will always pop up— you will never be completely free of them (sorry, I wish this weren't the case). But practicing awareness and diligence by asking good questions and teaching your brain new habits to move past those tendencies when they crop up can help you make progress and achieve your goals.

I Knew It

The brain gets what it expects. So, even if you have had issues with mindset work before (or think it's a bunch of mumbo-jumbo), I assure you it works. There is a reason the best athletes and top business moguls use visualization techniques.

If you try to implement the learnings in this book with a skeptical mind, your brain's confirmation bias (episode 102) and focusing illusion (episode 89) will combine to see the things that prove that to be right.

Remember the eleven million bits of information your subconscious is filtering through every second compared with the forty bits of the conscious brain? That means that, for every single item your subconscious lets through, 275,000 other things were determined not important enough. Is it possible that one (or 1,000) of them would have been evidence for the approach working?

When you are open to the possibility of something being different—when you are looking for the signs that this approach works—you will notice the things that prove that right (and ignore the other stuff that isn't serving you well).

Making the choice to believe in the power of these mind tricks will take some conscious work at the beginning but can quickly become a habit that helps you be successful in implementing behavioral economics and beyond.

Become a Curious Questioner

Take the next thirty days to look for the concepts you've learned about in this book. When you see an advertisement, stop to reflect on it.

- What are they trying to **nudge** you to do?

- How would the message change with a different **frame**?

- How could you include **reciprocity** to have a different outcome?

- If they don't have **social proof**, where would you add it?

- Would they benefit from breaking a **habit** or working with an existing one?

- If the **next step** isn't clear, how might you improve upon it?

- Where could you include a **story** element?

- Is the picture **priming** you in the right way?

Practicing curiosity on other work will train your brain to be curious in other areas. **It's good to ask questions.** This includes people who may question your new approach. Ask yourself why they feel that way—what can you learn from them?

It is helpful to pick up rocks and look from different angles. Combine thoughts to see what could be. And soon, you'll be doing this naturally with all your projects, work processes, and potential opportunities.

Congratulations, my friend! Your brain is now unlocked and you understand what your customer wants (even when they can't tell you). You can do this. You've got the tools you need to start applying behavioral economics in your life and business, and change your world.

Oh, and remember to *BE thoughtful.*

—Melina

Afterword

I truly hope you enjoyed all the insights, tips, and stories throughout *What Your Customer Wants and Can't Tell You*. And, because you now know the value of asking for things, giving generously, and social proof...I have a request:

- Will you rate and review this book on Amazon, GoodReads, Google, or any other platform you use?

- If you can think of one person who would enjoy the book, will you recommend it to them?

- If something resonated with you while reading—maybe you highlighted as you read, like I do—will you share it on social media and tag me, @thebrainybiz #WhatYourCustomerWants so I can connect with you?

Celebrating with listeners of *The Brainy Business* podcast and fans of *What Your Customer Wants and Can't Tell You* who have implemented their learnings and had successes is one of my favorite things. Got a question? Come ask me! I love chatting about behavioral economics and can't wait to have a great conversation with you.

If you're looking for more behavioral economics, please do visit *thebrainybusiness.com*—there are courses and lots of great content available for you there to continue your learning (including the free PDF workbook that accompanies this book at *thebrainybusiness.com/ApplyIt*) and learn more about how we can work together. You can also subscribe to *The Brainy Business* podcast, with new episodes every Friday. And, if you're ready to really dig in on applying this stuff (but don't want to be a professional researcher), the Certificate in Applied Behavioral Economics through the Texas A&M Human Behavior Laboratory could be a great fit for you. I'm honored to teach several of those courses and would love to work with you.

And, of course, if you are looking for a consultant or speaker on unlocking the brain to be more successful in business, email me: melina@thebrainybusiness.com.

I can't wait to connect with you, and thank you again.

BE thoughtful,

Melina

Acknowledgements

This book would not have been possible without the support and kindness of so many people and organizations. Thank you all for everything you have done to make this possible.

First and foremost, my husband Aaron. Thank you for your patience, for your support—for hours spent reading, providing feedback, finding citations, and being my rock. This could not have happened without you. And, of course, thank you to the rest of the family for your patience and understanding during the many late nights, missed meals, and time spent locked away with noise-cancelling headphones on.

To Dr. Marco Palma, Jeff Pool, and the rest of the Human Behavior Lab team at Texas A&M University—thank you for your faith in me and your continued support for myself and *The Brainy Business* (including technical review and citation support!). It means more than I can say.

To Roger Dooley, thank you for your kindness and support, and for being my forewordist—I am honored you agreed to support me in this way.

To Scott Miller—thank you for seeing something in me from a very early moment, and for pushing me in the right direction. Thank you for the advice, support, and connection to the wonderful team at Mango (and of course thank you to the Mango team!). Your kindness will never be forgotten.

And to everyone else who has helped shape *The Brainy Business* podcast and this book, *What Your Customer Wants and Can't Tell You*, by providing interviews, stories, time, support, sharing, listening, and so much more: thank you. There is not room here to list all the names, but I want to thank everyone quoted or otherwise represented in this book once more. In alphabetical order, thank you: Aline Holzwarth, April Vellacott, Bec Weeks, Benny Cheung (and the rest of the Dectech team), Binit Kumar, Brain Ahearn, Cristina McLamb, Dan Ariely, Elad Erdan, Elizabeth Immer, iMotions (the whole team), Gleb Tsipursky, Jennifer Clinehens, Jennifer Findlay, Jez Groom, Katy Milkman, Kwame Christian, Louise Ward, Mariel Court, Matt Wallaert, Michael Manniche, Michael Mazur, Nikki Rausch, Nir Eyal, Patrick Fagan, Richard Chataway, Samuel Salzer, Steve Alperin, Steve Wendel, Tim Houlihan, and Wendy Wood.

Last, but not least, thank you to all the listeners, subscribers, sharers, and supporters of *The Brainy Business* podcast. Without you, none of this would be here. Thank you.

Notes

1   Kaku, M. (2014, August 20). The golden age of neuroscience has arrived. *Wall Street Journal*. Retrieved from: www.wsj.com/articles/michio-kaku-the-golden-age-of-neuroscience-has-arrived-1408577023.

2   Kahneman, D. (2011). *Thinking, fast and slow*. Farrar, Straus and Giroux.

3   Pradeep, A.K. (2010). *The buying brain: Secrets for selling to the subconscious mind*. John Wiley & Sons.

4   Pradeep, A.K. (2010). *The buying brain: Secrets for selling to the subconscious mind*. John Wiley & Sons.

5   Ash, T. (2021). Unleash your primal brain: Demystifying how we think and why we act. Morgan James Publishing.

6   There is an ever-growing number of studies within the fields of behavioral economics and behavioral science from around the world, which I expect to grow faster in the coming years. I highly recommend *behavioraleconomics.com* as a starting resource for anyone looking for more academic research from the field.

7   Steidl, P. (2014). *Neurobranding* (2nd ed.) CreateSpace. Page 15.

8   Kahneman, D., Slovic, P., & Tversky, A. (Eds.) (1982). *Judgement under uncertainty: Heuristics and biases*. Cambridge University Press.

9   Biddle, G. (2018, April 2017). How Netflix's customer obsession created a customer obsession. *Medium*.

10 Nisbett, R., & Wilson, T. D. (1977). The Halo Effect: Evidence for unconscious alteration of judgments. *Journal of Personality and Social Psychology, 35*, 250–256.

11 Bourtchouladze, R. (2002). *Memories are made of this: How memory works in humans and animals*. Columbia University Press.

12 Palmer, M. (Host). (2019, May 17). An overview of memory biases. (No. 48) [Audio podcast episode]. In *The Brainy Business*.

13 Gardner, R. W. & Lohrenz, L. J. (1960). Leveling-Sharpening and Serial Reproduction of a Story. *Bulletin of the Menninger Clinic, 24*(6), 295.

14 Arkowitz, H., & Lilienfeld, S. O. (2010, January 1). Why Science Tells Us Not to Rely on Eyewitness Accounts. *Scientific American*. www.scientificamerican.com/article/do-the-eyes-have-it Note: the language of the story getting lost in the mall is one I wrote for the example within the book, and is not the exact language used by the researchers in the study.

15 Begg, I. M., Anas, A., & Farinacci, S. (1992). Dissociation of processes in belief: Source recollection, statement familiarity, and the illusion of truth. *Journal of Experimental Psychology: General, 121*(4), 446–458.

16 Nickerson, R. S. (1998). Confirmation bias: A ubiquitous phenomenon in many guises. *Review of General Psychology, 2*(2), 175–220.

17 Haidt, J. (2006). *The happiness hypothesis: Finding modern truth in ancient wisdom*. Basic Books.

18 Bergland, C. (2019). The neurochemicals of happiness. *Psychology Today*.; Palmer, M. (Host). (2020, October 23). Get your D.O.S.E. of brain chemicals. (No. 123) [Audio podcast episode]. In *The Brainy Business*.

19 Zaltman, G. (2003). *How customers think: Essential insights into the mind of the market*. Harvard Business School Press.

20   FORA.tv. (2011, March 2). *Dopamine jackpot! Sapolsky on the science of pleasure* [Video]. YouTube. www.youtube.com/watch?v=axrywDP9Ii0; Weinschenk, S. (2015, October 22). Shopping, dopamine, and anticipation. *Psychology Today.*

21   Ramachandran, V. (2009, November). *The neurons that shaped civilization* [Video]. TED Conferences. www.ted.com/talks/vilayanur_ramachandran_the_neurons_that_shaped_civilization; Palmer, M. (Host). (2019, January 18). Mirror neurons: A fascinating discovery from a monkey, a hot day, and an ice cream cone. (No. 31) [Audio podcast episode]. In *The Brainy Business.*

22   di Pellegrino, G., Fadiga, L., Fogassi, L., Gallese V. & Rizzolatti, G. (1992). Understanding motor events: a neurophysiological study. Experimental Brain Research, 91, 176–180.; Gallese, V., Fadiga, L., Fogassi, L., & Rizzolatti, G. (1996). Action recognition in the premotor cortex, *Brain,* 119(2), 593–609.

23   Iacoboni M, Molnar-Szakacs I, Gallese V, Buccino G, Mazziotta JC, & Rizzolatti G. (2005) Grasping the Intentions of Others with One's Own Mirror Neuron System. *PLoS Biology, 3(3):* e79.

24   Goel, V. (2014, June 29). Facebook tinkers with users' emotions in news feed experiment, stirring outcry. *The New York Times.*

25   Sharot, T. (2012, February). *The optimism bias* [Video]. TED Conferences. www.ted.com/talks/tali_sharot_the_optimism_bias; Palmer, M. (Host). (2019, February 8). Optimism bias: The good and the bad of those rose-colored glasses. (No. 34) [Audio podcast episode]. In *The Brainy Business.*

26   Palmer, M. (Host). (2019, April 26). Overview of personal biases. (No. 45) [Audio podcast episode]. In *The Brainy Business.* Palmer, M. (Host). (2019, May 3). Biases toward others—including groups. (No. 46) [Audio podcast episode]. In *The Brainy Business.*

27   Samuelson, W., & Zeckhauser, R. J. (1988). Status quo bias in decision making. *Journal of Risk and Uncertainty, 1,* 7–59.

28   Meakin, L. (2019, December 29). Top jobs for next decade are behavioral scientist, data analyst. *Bloomberg.*

29   Sutherland, R. (2019). *Alchemy: The dark art and curious science of creating magic in brands, business, and life.* HarperCollins.

30   Learn more about the Right Question Institute and questionstorming at rightquestion.org.

31   Berger, W. (2016). *A more beautiful question: The power of inquiry to spark breakthrough ideas.* Bloomsbury USA.

32   Lang, N. (2013, September 2). 31 famous quotations you've been getting wrong. *Thought Catalog.*

33   Kahneman, D. (2011). *Thinking, fast and slow.* Farrar, Straus and Giroux.

34   Staff. (2007, August 10). 'Cozy' or tiny? How to decode real estate ads. *Today.* www.today.com/news/cozy-or-tiny-how-decode-real-estate-ads-wbna20215090.

35   Lawson, M. (2018, September 24). #1003: How CoastHills Credit Union achieved modern marketing success with an old idea...CUBroadcast.

36   Terao, Y., Fukuda, H., & Hikosaka, O. (2017). What do eye movements tell us about patients with neurological disorders?—An introduction to saccade recording in the clinical setting. *Proceedings of the Japan Academy. Series B, Physical and Biological Sciences,* 93(10), 772–801.

37   Goldstein, D. G. (2007, March). Getting attention for unrecognized brands. *Harvard Business Review.* Janiszewski, C. (1993). Preattentive mere exposure effects. *Journal of Consumer Research,* 20(3), 376–392.

38   Pradeep, A.K. (2010). *The buying brain: Secrets for selling to the subconscious mind.* John Wiley & Sons.

39   Burmester, A. (2015, November 5). How do our brains reconstruct the visual world? *The Conversation.* theconversation.com/how-do-our-brains-reconstruct-the-visual-world-49276.

40   Kay, A., Wheeler, S., Bargh, J., & Ross, L. (2004). Material priming: The influence of mundane physical objects on situational construal and competitive behavioral choice. *Organizational Behavior and Human Decision Processes, 95,* 83–96. This study has not been replicated by others. However, I have chosen to still include the study to show how the literal association within the brain works, and get you thinking about how this can impact your business via image and word choice.

41   Fitzsimons, G. M., Chartrand, T. L., & Fitzsimons, G. J. (2008). Automatic effects of brand exposure on motivated behavior: How Apple makes you "think different." *Journal of Consumer Research, 35*(1), 21–35.

42   Eveleth, R. (2013, December). How do we smell? [Video]. TED Conferences. www.ted.com/talks/rose_eveleth_how_do_we_smell.

43   Aqrabawi, A.J., & Kim, J.C. (2018). Hippocampal projections to the anterior olfactory nucleus differentially convey spatiotemporal information during episodic odour memory. *Nature Communications, 9*, 2735.

44   ScentAir is not the only scent branding company around. I chose to include them because of the assortment of stats and research on their page which, at the time of publication, included the stats listed in this section. See more on their website, scentair.com/how-it-works.

45   Holland, R. W., Hendriks, M., & Aarts, H. (2005). Smells like clean spirit: Nonconscious effects of scent on cognition and behavior. *Psychological Science, 16*(9), 689–693.

46   Pradeep, A.K. (2010). *The buying brain: Secrets for selling to the subconscious mind.* John Wiley & Sons.

47   Hirsch, A. (1995). Effects of ambient odors on slot-machine usage in a Las Vegas casino. *Psychology and Marketing, 12*(7), 585–594.

48   Hirsch, A. R. (1990). "Preliminary Results of Olfaction Nike Study," note dated November 16 distributed by the Smell and Taste Treatment and Research Foundation, Ltd. Chicago, IL. Bone, P.F., & Jantrania, S. (1992). Olfaction as a cue for product quality. *Marketing Letters, 3*, 289–296.

49   Staff. (2011, August 16). The smell of commerce: How companies use scents to sell their products. *The Independent.*

50   Hagan, P. (2012, October 31). How the aroma of freshly baked bread makes us kinder to strangers. *The Daily Mail.*

51   Moss, M., & Oliver, L. (2012). Plasma 1,8-cineole correlates with cognitive performance following exposure to rosemary essential oil aroma. *Therapeutic Advances in Psychopharmacology*, 103–113.

52   Staff. (2009, February 16). ScentAir launches the sweet smell of success. *Retail Technology Review.*

53   Redd, W. H., Manne, S. L., Peters, B., Jacobsen, P. B., & Schmidt, H. (1994). Fragrance administration to reduce anxiety during MR imaging. *Journal of Magnetic Resonance Imaging, 4*(4), 623–626.

54   Kotler, P. (1974). Atmospherics as a Marketing Tool. *Journal of Retailing. 49*(4), 48–64.

55   Vida, I., Obadia, C., & Kunz, M. (2007). The effects of background music on consumer responses in a high-end supermarket. *International Review of Retail Distribution and Consumer Research,* (5), 469–482.

56   Vida, I., Obadia, C., & Kunz, M. (2007). The effects of background music on consumer responses in a high-end supermarket. *International Review of Retail Distribution and Consumer Research,* (5), 469–482.

57   Vida, I., Obadia, C., & Kunz, M. (2007). The effects of background music on consumer responses in a high-end supermarket. *International Review of Retail Distribution and Consumer Research,* (5), 469–482.

58   North, A., Hargreaves, D., & McKendrick, J., (1997), In-store music affects product choice. *Nature, 390*, 132.

59   eBay Press Release. (2014, October 27). Radio, chatter and football—the sounds that help us shop. www.ebayinc.com/stories/press-room/uk/radio-chatter-and-football-the-sounds-that-help-us-shop.

60   Peck, J. & Shu, S. B. (2009). The effect of mere touch on perceived ownership. *Journal of Consumer Research, 36*(3), 434–434.

61   Keysers, C., Wicker, B., Gazzola, V., Anton, J., Fogassi, L., & Gallese, V. (2004). A touching sight: SII/PV activation during the observation and experience of touch. *Neuron, 42*(2), 335–346.

62   Williams, L. E. & Bargh, J. A. (2008). Experiencing physical warmth promotes interpersonal warmth. *Science, 322*(5901), 606–607. This study has not been replicated by others. However, I have chosen to still include the study to show how the literal association within the brain works, and get you thinking about how this can impact your business via image and word choice.

63   Steidl, P. (2014). *Neurobranding* (2nd ed.) CreateSpace.

64   Bargh, J. A., Chen, M., & Burrows, L. (1996). Automaticity of social behavior: Direct effects of trait construct and stereotype activation on action, *Journal of Personality and Social Psychology 71*(2), 230–244. This study has not been replicated by others. However, I have chosen to still include the study to show how the literal association within the brain works, and get you thinking about how this can impact your business via image and word choice.

65 Steele, J. R. & Ambady, N. (2006). "Math is hard!" The effect of gender priming on women's attitudes. *Journal of Experimental Social Psychology 42*(4), 428–436.

66 Zhong, C. & Liljenquist, K., (2006), Washing away your sins: threatened morality and physical cleansing, *Science, 313* (5792), 1451–1452.

67 Tversky, A., & Kahneman, D. (1974). Judgment under uncertainty: Heuristics and biases. *Science (New Series), 185,* 1124–1131.

68 Ariely, D. (2010). *Predictably irrational: The hidden forces that shape our decisions.* HarperCollins.

69 Wansink, B., Kent, R., & Hoch, S. (1998). An Anchoring and Adjustment Model of Purchase Quantity Decisions. *Journal of Marketing Research, 35*(1), 71–81.

70 Palmer, M. (2019, March 14). 1 word that increased sales by 38 percent. *CUInsight.*

71 Ahearn, B., (2019), Influence people: Powerful everyday opportunities to persuade that are lasting and ethical, Influence People, LLC. Palmer, M. (Host). (2020, June 12). How to ethically influence people: Interview with author Brian Ahearn. (No. 104) [Audio podcast episode]. In *The Brainy Business.*

72 Ariely, D. (2010). *Predictably irrational: The hidden forces that shape our decisions.* HarperCollins.

73 Simonson, I. (1993). Get closer to your customers by understanding how they make choices. *California Management Review, 35*(4) pp. 68–84.

74 Bleich, S. N., Barry, C. L., Gary-Webb, T. L., & Herring, B. J. (2014). Reducing sugar-sweetened beverage consumption by providing caloric information: How Black adolescents alter their purchases and whether the effects persist. *American Journal of Public Health, 104,* 2417–2424.

75 Miller, A. M. (2019, May 28). A graphic comparing a bottle of soda to 6 donuts is going viral and it's making people want to eat more pastries. *Insider.*

76 Kahneman, D. & Tversky, A. (1979). Prospect theory: An analysis of decision under risk. *Econometrica, 47,* 263–291.

77 When sharing this example (of putting $50 in someone's account and "removing" it if they don't perform the actions), I have sometimes gotten questions or concerns about deceptive practices and causing people to overdraw their accounts. This money would only be in the Current Balance (not Available Balance), so no one would be able to spend the money and incur fees or anything. Seeing it in the Current Balance triggers the brain to want to move it into the Available Balance. If you are unfamiliar with what I am talking about, log into your online banking and look for these terms. When something is on hold—say you make a large deposit or use your card at a hotel—the Current and Available Balances will be different. You can only spend what is in your Available Balance.

78 The sales team incentives example from Binit Kumar was provided to me directly via email.

79 Biswas, D. & Grau, S.L. (2008). Consumer choices under product option framing: Loss aversion principles or sensitivity to price differentials? *Psychology & Marketing, 25*(5), 399–415.

80 Information from the app interrupts program was provided to me directly from Aline Holzwarth via personal interview and email of materials. The following article is provided for additional information. Holzwarth, A. (2018, September 19). How commitment devices can help people stick to their health goals. *Pattern Health.*

81 Tsai, Y.-F. L. & Kaufman, D. M. (2009). The socioemotional effects of a computer-simulated animal on children's empathy and humane attitudes. *Journal of Educational Computing Research, 41*(1), 103–122.

82 Information on how Pattern Health has used "Virgil the Turtle" as well as images (and permission to use them within this book) were provided to me by Aline Holzwarth, via personal interview and email exchange.

83 Wright, C. (2020, June 20). Craigslist, back rooms & money launderers: Two months hunting for the world's most wanted bourbon. *Gear Patrol.* www.gearpatrol.com/food/drinks/a638762/how-to-buy-pappy-van-winkle-bourbon.

84 Lee, S. Y. & Seidle, R. (2012). Narcissists as consumers: The effects of perceived scarcity on processing of product information. *Social Behavior and Personality, 40*(9), 1485–1499.

85 Mullainathan, S. & Shafir, E. (2013). *Scarcity: Why having too little means so much.* Time Books.

86 Akçay, Y., Boyacı, T. & Zhang, D. (2013). Selling with money-back guarantees: The impact on prices, quantities, and retail profitability. *Production and Operations Management, 22*(4), 777–791.

87 Starbucks has stopped using their accounts like @therealPSL and @Frappuccino. They now only use their main account for all postings.

88 A. P. Kirman. (1993). Ants, rationality and recruitment. *Quarterly Journal of Economics, 108*(1), 137–156.

89 Price, M. E. (2013, June 25). Human herding: How people are like guppies. *Psychology Today.*

90 Palmer, M. (Host). (2019, January 11). Booms, Bubbles, and Busts. (No. 30) [Audio podcast episode]. In *The Brainy Business.*

91 Asch, S. (1955). Opinions and social pressure. *Scientific American, 193*(5), 31–35.

92 Goldstein, N. J., Martin, S. J., & Cialdini, R. B. (2010). *Yes! 50 scientifically proven ways to be persuasive.* Robert B. Cialdini. New York: Free Press.

93 Influenceatwork. (2012, November 26). *Science of Persuasion* [Video]. YouTube. www.youtube.com/watch?v=cFdCzN7RYbw.

94 Sunstein, C.R. (2013). *Simpler: The future of government.* Simon & Schuster. Thaler, R.H. & Sunstein, C.R. (2008). *Nudge: Improving decisions about health, wealth, and happiness.* Penguin Books.

95 Young, L. (2016, September 13). Watch these awkward elevator rides from an old episode of candid camera. *Atlas Obscura.*

96 Cialdini, R. B. (2007). *Influence: The psychology of persuasion (Revised).* HarperCollins.

97 Bekk, M. & Sporrle, M. (2010). The influence of perceived personality characteristics on positive attitude toward and suitability of a celebrity as a marketing campaign endorser. *The Open Psychology Journal, 3*(1), 54–66.

98 To learn more about Niche Skincare, visit nicheskincare.com or see the social proof on their Instagram, @nicheskincare.

99 Behavioural Economics Team of the Australian Government (BETA). (2017, October 16). Nudge vs superbugs: A behavioural economics trial to reduce the overprescribing of antibiotics. Retrieved from: behaviouraleconomics.pmc.gov.au/sites/default/files/projects/report-nudge-vs-superbugs.pdf.

100 Thaler, R.H. & Sunstein, C.R. (2008). *Nudge: Improving decisions about health, wealth, and happiness.* Penguin Books.

101 Thaler, R., & Benartzi, S. (2004). Save more tomorrow™: Using behavioral economics to increase employee saving. *Journal of Political Economy, 112*(S1), S164-S187.

102 Thaler, R.H. & Sunstein, C.R. (2008). *Nudge: Improving decisions about health, wealth, and happiness.* Penguin Books.

103 Thaler, R. H., Sunstein, C. R., & Balz, J. P. (2012) Choice Architecture. The Behavioral Foundations of Public Policy, Ch. 25, Eldar Shafir, ed. (2012). Available at SSRN: ssrn.com/abstract=2536504 or dx.doi.org/10.2139/ssrn.2536504.

104 Staff. (2009, October 22). *52 percent opted to donate to state parks in September.* Washington Policy Center.

105 Thaler, R.H. & Sunstein, C.R. (2008). *Nudge: Improving decisions about health, wealth, and happiness.* Penguin Books.

106 Thaler, R. (2010, January 11). Measuring the LSD effect: 36 percent improvement. *Nudge Blog.*

107 Thaler, R. (2008, August 6). A car pedal for the lead foot in your family. *Nudge Blog.*

108 Thaler, R. H., Sunstein, C. R., & Balz, J. P. (2012) Choice Architecture. The Behavioral Foundations of Public Policy, Ch. 25, Eldar Shafir, ed. (2012). Available at SSRN: ssrn.com/abstract=2536504 or dx.doi.org/10.2139/ssrn.2536504.

109 Blog. (2018, February 7). How many daily decisions do we make? *Science.*

110 Shiv, B., & Fedorikhin, A. (1999). Heart and Mind in Conflict: The Interplay of Affect and Cognition in Consumer Decision Making. *Journal of Consumer Research, 26*(3), 278–292.

111 Edland A. & Svenson O. (1993) Judgment and decision making under time pressure. In: Svenson O., Maule A.J. (eds) Time Pressure and Stress in Human Judgment and Decision Making. Springer, Boston, MA.

112 Margalit, L. (2019, November 5). This is your brain on sale. *CMS Wire.*

113 Ordóñez, L. & Benson, L. (1997). Decisions under time pressure: How time constraint affects risky decision making. Organizational Behavior and Human Decision Processes, 71(2), 121–140.

114 Amabile, T.M., Noonan Hadley, C., & Kramer, S.J. (2002). Creativity under the gun. *Harvard Business Review.*

115 Giblin, C.E., Morewedge, C.K. & Norton, M.I. (2013, September 16). Unexpected benefits of deciding by mind wandering. Frontier Psychology, Volume 4, Article 598.

116 Chataway, R. (2020). *The behaviour business: How to apply behavioural science for business success.* Harriman House.

117 Dooley, R., (2019), Friction: The untapped force that can be your most powerful advantage. McGraw-Hill Education.

118 Cheema, A., & Soman, D. (2008). The effect of partitions on controlling consumption. *Journal of Marketing Research, 45*(6), 665–675.

119 Rolls, B.J., Morris, E.L., & Roe, L.S. (2002). Portion size of food affects energy intake in normal-weight and overweight men and women. *The American Journal of Clinical Nutrition, 76*(6), 1207–1213.

120 Dooley, R. (n.d.). The psychology of beer (and wine too). *Neuromarketing Blog.*

121 Cheema, A., & Soman, D. (2008). The effect of partitions on controlling consumption. *Journal of Marketing Research, 45*(6), 665–675.

122 Bettinger, E., Cunha, N., Lichand, G., & Madeira, R. (2020). Are the effects of informational interventions driven by salience? University of Zurich, Department of Economics, Working Paper No. 350.

123 Cheema, A., & Soman, D. (2008). The effect of partitions on controlling consumption. *Journal of Marketing Research, 45*(6), 665–675.

124 Soman, D. & Cheema, A. (2011). Earmarking and partitioning: Increasing saving by low-income households. *Journal of Marketing Research, 48*, S14-S22.

125 Dhar, R., Huber, J., & Khan, U. (2007). The shopping momentum effect. *Journal of Marketing Research, 44*(3), 370–378.

126 Morwitz, V.G., Johnson, E., & Schmittlein, D. (1993). Does measuring intent change behavior? *Journal of Consumer Research, 20*(1), 46–61.

127 Kaplan, K. (1997, January 15). 5 customers sue AOL over new unlimited access plan. *LA Times.* Brown, M. (n.d.) AOL goes unlimited. *This Day In Tech History.*

128 Mazar, N., Plassmann, H., Robitaille, N. & Lindner, A. (2016). Pain of paying?—A metaphor gone literal: Evidence from neural and behavioral science. Rotman School of Management Working Paper No. 2901808, INSEAD Working Paper No. 2017/06/MKT.

129 Kamat, P., Hogan, C., (2019, January 28), How Uber leverages applied behavioral economics at scale, Uber Engineering Blog. Uber ExpressPOOL eng.uber.com/applied-behavioral-science-at-scale.

130 Zellermayer, O. (1996). The pain of paying. (Doctoral dissertation). Department of Social and Decision Sciences, Carnegie Mellon University, Pittsburgh, PA.

131 Rick, S., Cryder, C. E., & Loewenstein, G. (2008). Tightwads and spendthrifts: An interdisciplinary review, *Journal of Consumer Research 34*(6), 767–782.

132 Prelec, D., & Loewenstein, G. (1998). The red and the black: Mental accounting of savings and debt. *Marketing Science, 17*(1), 4–28.

133 Coulter, K.S., Choi, P., & Monroe, K.B. (2012). Comma n' cents in pricing: The effects of auditory representation encoding on price magnitude perceptions. *Journal of Consumer Psychology, 22*(3), 395–407.

134 Prelec, D., & Loewenstein, G. (1998). The red and the black: Mental accounting of savings and debt. *Marketing Science, 17*(1), 4–28.

135 The story of Klingon in the Bing Translator was provided to me directly by Matt Wallaert via phone interview. He was also a guest on The Brainy Business episode 128, where we talked about it briefly, and you can learn more about his research in his book: Wallaert, M. (2019). *Start at the end: How to build products that create change.* Penguin Publishing Group.

136 Berman, B. (2005). How to delight your customers. *California Management Review, 48*(1), 129–151.

137 This chart I've created for the book is adapted from the one in the article referenced above, How to delight customers.

138 Berman, B. (2005). How to delight your customers. *California Management Review, 48*(1), 129–151.

139 Coyne, K.P. (1989). Beyond service fads—Meaningful strategies for the real world. Sloan Management Review, 30(4), 69–76; Dick, A.S. & Basu, K. (1994). Customer loyalty: Toward an integrated conceptual framework. Journal of the Academy of Marketing Science, 22, 99–113.; T.A. Oliva, T.A., Oliver, R.L., & Macmillan, I.C. (1992). A catastrophe model for developing service satisfaction strategies. *Journal of Marketing, 56*(3), 83–98.

140 Berman, B. (2005). How to delight your customers. *California Management Review, 48*(1), 129–151.

141 Berman, B. (2005). How to delight your customers. *California Management Review, 48*(1), 129–151.

142 Reichheld, F.F. & Sasser Jr., W.E. (1990). "Zero defections: Quality comes to services," Harvard Business Review, 68(5), 105–111.

143 Heskett, J.L. (2002). Beyond customer loyalty. *Journal of Service Theory and Practice, 12*(6), 355–357.

144 Chubb, H. (2019, June 6). Ed Sheeran teams up with Heinz ketchup to create 'Edchup.' *People.*

145 Berman, B. (2005). How to delight your customers. *California Management Review, 48*(1), 129–151.

146 Fredrickson, B. L. & Kahneman, D. (1993). Duration neglect in retrospective evaluations of affective episodes. *Journal of Personality and Social Psychology, 65*(1), 45–55.

147 Redelmeier, D.A., Katz, J. & Kahneman, D. (2003). Memories of a colonoscopy: A randomized trial. *Pain, 104*(1–2), 187–94.

148 Kahneman, D., Fredrickson, B., Schreiber, C., & Redelmeier, D. (1993). When more pain is preferred to less: Adding a better end. *Psychological Science, 4*(6), 401–405.

149 Wood, W., (2019), *Good habits, bad habits: The science of making positive changes. Farrar, Straus and Giroux.*

150 Wood, W. & Neal, D.T. (2009). *The habitual consumer. Journal of Consumer Psychology, 19*(4), 579–592. Zaltman, G. (2003). *How customers think: essential insights into the mind of the market. Harvard Business Press.*

151 *Eyal, N., & Hoover, R. (2014). Hooked: How to build habit-forming products. Portfolio/Penguin.*

152 Details on Pique were provided via direct interview with cofounder, Bec Weeks, in episode 119 of *The Brainy Business* podcast.

153 Milkman, K. L., Minson, J. A., & Volpp, K. G. (2014). Holding The Hunger Games hostage at the gym: An evaluation of temptation bundling. *Management Science, 60*(2), 283–299.

154 Lorre, C., et. al (Writers), & Cendrowski, M. (Director). (2008, December 15). The bath item gift hypothesis [Television Series Episode] In L. Aronsohn(Producer), *The Big Bang Theory.* Columbia Broadcasting System.

155 The 6 Principles of Persuasion by Dr. Robert Cialdini [Official Site]. (2019, June 25). www.influenceatwork. com/principles-of-persuasion.

156 Freedman, J.L. & Fraser, S.C. (1966). Compliance without pressure: The foot-in-the-door technique. *Journal of Personality and Social Psychology, 4*(2), 195–202. Markman, A. (2008, October 12). The power of yard signs II: Escalation of commitment. *Psychology Today.*

157 If you're in the market for amazing branded photos for your business, I highly recommend Jennifer Findlay Portraiture. My headshots at the time of this publication were done by Jennifer and she is phenomenal to work with.

158 Cialdini, R.B., et. al. (1975). Reciprocal concessions procedure for inducing compliance: The door-in-the-face technique. *Journal of Personality and Social Psychology, 31*(2), 206–215.

159 Note, this book is focused on fifteen to twenty of more than two hundred brain concepts to help you learn the process of applying behavioral economics to business. Those others can be your spices and seasonings as you start experimenting.

160 Details about The Littery were provided to me directly via an interview with CEO Michael Manniche in episode 75 of *The Brainy Business* podcast.

161 This is also triggering a loop of prefactual / counterfactual thinking, which are essentially when we "what if" and "why not." While not part of this book, both have episodes on *The Brainy Business* podcast, 68 and 71.

162 Buehler, J. (2017, October 19). Dogs really can smell your fear, and then they get scared, too. *NewScientist*.

163 Nelson, N. (2016, May 3). The power of a picture. *Netflix Blog*. Roettgers, J. (2016, January 7), This simple trick helped Netflix increase video viewing by more than 20 percent. *Variety*.

164 Kahneman, D. (2011). *Thinking, fast and slow*. Farrar, Straus and Giroux.

165 Lam, B. (2015, January 30). The psychological difference between $12.00 and $11.67. *The Atlantic*.

166 Wadhwa, M. & Zhang, K. (2014). This number just feels right: The impact of roundedness of price numbers on product evaluations. *Journal of Consumer Research, 41*(5), 1172–1185.

167 Ariely, D. (2008). *Predictably irrational: The hidden forces that shape our decisions*. HarperCollins.

168 Hanson, R. (2009, January 10). Why we like middle options, small menus. *Overcoming Bias*.

169 Graff, F. (2018, February 7). How many daily decisions do we make? *Science*.

170 Brian explained this example while being interviewed on episode 104 of *The Brainy Business* podcast. You can find more of his work in his book: Ahearn, B. (2019). *Influence PEOPLE: Powerful everyday opportunities to persuade that are lasting and ethical*. Influence People, LLC.

171 Mitrokostas, S. (2019, January 14). Why cereal boxes are at eye level with kids. *Insider*.

172 Cobe, P. (2020, September 25). Texas restaurants turn to neuroscience for menu makeovers. *Restaurant Business*.

173 Witte, K. (2019, November 20). Local businesses use Texas A&M behavior science to design menus. *KBTX*.

174 Details for the menu project were provided via an interview with Jez Groom and April Vellacott; they also provided permission to use the images in the book at that time. You can hear my interview with them on episode 131 of The Brainy Business podcast, and check out their book: Groom, J. & Vellacott, A. (2020). *Ripple: The big effects of small behaviour changes in business*. Harriman House.

175 Trafton, A. (2014, January 16). In the blink of an eye. *MIT News*. Staff, (2019, March 6), Mobile Marketing Association reveals brands need a "first second strategy." *Mobile Marketing Association*.

176 Sunstein, C. (2020, May 19). How to make coronavirus restrictions easier to swallow. *Bloomberg*.

177 Details on the project and permission to use the imagery in this book were provided via an interview with Elizabeth Immer from Zuzanna Krzyzanska for The Ergonomen Usability. To read more about the project with Swisscom, read this: Immer, E. (2020, March 6). A "fresh" start for collections at Swisscom. *Ergonomen*.

178 Celletti, C. (2020, June 25). Conversations that matter—Nudgestock 2020: Necessity is the mother of reinvention. *Ogilvy*.

179 Details on Shapa were provided via a direct interview with Dan Ariely, which you can hear on episode 101 of The Brainy Business podcast and approved by his team to appear in this book. Learn more about Shapa at www.shapa.com.

180 Sunstein, C. (2020, May 19). How to make coronavirus restrictions easier to swallow. *Bloomberg*.

181 Petreycik, C. (2019, July 10). Cotton candy grape watch: Which stores have them now. *Food and Wine*.

182 Zak, P. (2014, October 28). Why your brain loves good storytelling. Harvard Business Review.

183 Staff. (2020, January 24). Storytelling and cultural traditions. *National Geographic*.

184 The Colu team provided me with details from the Jerusalem Boulevard project via a direct interview, and you can also hear about it on episode 113 of The Brainy Business podcast. They also provided the imagery and permission to use it, as well as the story, in this book. Learn more about the project here: Staff. (2020, January 1), Urban regeneration In TLV—Jerusalem Boulevard, Colu. colu.com/case-studies/urban-regeneration-in-tel-aviv-colu-civic-engagement.

185 Staff. (2020). Cancer Facts & Figures 2020. Cancer.org.

186 Details provided via direct interview with Survivornet CEO, Scott Alperin, as well as permission to include the story in this book. Learn more about them at www.survivornet.com.

187 Zhang, Y. (2015, November 2). The registration test results Netflix never expected. *Apptimize*.

188 Watson, A. (2020, November 10). Number of Netflix paid subscribers worldwide from 3rd quarter 2011 to 3rd quarter 2020. *Statista*.

189 Details on the Dectech research was provided to me via direct interviews with the team, some of which you can hear on episode 140 of *The Brainy Business* podcast. Read the research here: Mitchell, T. & Benny, C. (2020). Using behavioural science to reduce opportunistic insurance fraud. *Applied Marketing Analytics, 5*(4), 294–303.

190 Details provided via direct interview, which you can hear in episode 116 of *The Brainy Business* podcast, also check out his book: Wendel, S. (2020). *Designing for behavior change: Applying psychology and behavioral economics* (2nd Ed). O'Reilly Media.

191 Nelson, N. (2016, May 3). The power of a picture. *Netflix Blog*.

192 Hern, A. (2014, February 5). Why Google has 200m reasons to put engineers over designers. The Guardian.

193 Palmer, M. (Host). (2019, May 17). Color theory. (No. 61) [Audio podcast episode]. In *The Brainy Business*.

194 Chataway, R. (2020). *The behaviour business: How to apply behavioural science for business success.* Harriman House.

195 Learn more about the Texas A&M Human Behavior Lab (including information about signing up for our Certificate in Applied Behavioral Economics at hbl.tamu.edu/certificate-program.

196 Details about iMotions were approved by members of their team, including their inclusion in this book. For more details about them, visit www.imotions.com.

197 Sundararajan, R.R., Palma, M.A. & Pourahmadi, M. (2017). Reducing brain signal noise in the prediction of economic choices: A case study in neuroeconomics. *Frontiers in Neuroscience, 11,* 704.

198 Sunstein, C. (2013). *Simpler: The future of government.* Simon & Schuster.

199 Rose, J. (2019, April 1). Benefits of using your opposite hand—Grow brain cells while brushing your teeth. *Good Financial Cents.*

200 Coyier, C. (2016, January 8). What is bikeshedding?. CSS-Tricks.

201 Eyal, N. & Li-Eyal, J. (2019). *Indistractable: How to control your attention and choose your life.* BenBella Books, Inc.

About the Author

Melina Palmer is founder and CEO of The Brainy Business, which provides behavioral economics consulting to businesses of all sizes from around the world. Her award-winning podcast, *The Brainy Business: Understanding the Psychology of Why People Buy*, has downloads in over 160 countries and is used as a resource for applying behavioral economics for many universities and businesses. A lifelong learner, Melina obtained her master's in behavioral economics from The Chicago School of Professional Psychology and loves teaching applied behavioral economics through the Texas A&M Human Behavior Lab. A member of the Global Association of Applied Behavioral Scientists, she has contributed research to the Association for Consumer Research, Filene Research Institute, and runs the Behavioral Economics and Business column for *Inc.* magazine.

Mango Publishing, established in 2014, publishes an eclectic list of books by diverse authors—both new and established voices—on topics ranging from business, personal growth, women's empowerment, LGBTQ studies, health, and spirituality to history, popular culture, time management, decluttering, lifestyle, mental wellness, aging, and sustainable living. We were recently named 2019 *and* 2020's #1 fastest growing independent publisher by *Publishers Weekly*. Our success is driven by our main goal, which is to publish high-quality books that will entertain readers as well as make a positive difference in their lives.

Our readers are our most important resource; we value your input, suggestions, and ideas. We'd love to hear from you—after all, we are publishing books for you!

Please stay in touch with us and follow us at:

Facebook: Mango Publishing
Twitter: @MangoPublishing
Instagram: @MangoPublishing
LinkedIn: Mango Publishing
Pinterest: Mango Publishing

Newsletter: mangopublishinggroup.com/newsletter

Join us on Mango's journey to reinvent publishing, one book at a time.

9 781642 505627